salad

break

salad
freak

recipes to feed a healthy obsession

jess damuck

foreword by martha stewart

PHOTOGRAPHY BY LINDA PUGLIESE

ABRAMS, NEW YORK

for
r. remmey
bumsted iv,
with love.

i am thinking
of you every time
i cook,

which is to say,

always.

contents

by martha stewart

When a cookbook author or chef asks me to review, write a blurb, or compose a foreword for a new book, I request a galley or an early copy. Then I wait until I am very hungry to open it and start to read. If I immediately begin to salivate, make mental notes about this or that, or dog-ear pages for future reference, I know I am going to like the book, and I know the readers who buy it are going to be pleased to try many of the recipes. This is what happened immediately with *Salad Freak*. Jess Damuck's first book is a pure joy to look at, to read, and to cook from.

I have known Jess for several years—in fact, she worked in the test kitchens and on the television sets of *Martha Stewart Living*. Dressed in her signature, colorful (primarily acid yellow) cotton jumpsuits, with her straight dark brown hair caught in an unruly ponytail, she was always serious about any task she had to undertake, thorough in her preparation, and fastidious without being fussy about her presentation of each and every recipe.

This book is full of practical, smart, and sometimes unusual solutions to a vast subject matter—the matter being SALADS: their ingredients, their preparation, their seasoning, their dressing, and their serving.

I happen to crave salads and eat at least one each day. Many of these recipes caused me to rethink combinations of ingredients—the incorporation of fruits, vegetables, herbs, nuts, spices, dairy products, and even meats and fish into one-dish wonders. I now have a whole new encyclopedia of combinations to last me many months and even years, for the mix-and-match approach really is limitless when it comes to making a salad.

The valuable glossaries—lists of pantry staples, dressings, fresh ingredients, etc.—are imperative to read and remember. And the glorious photography captures the essence of each salad, as well as clearly illustrating each and every ingredient contained in that salad. Jess is a very accomplished artist/illustrator/art director—skills she has been honing her whole life! And the no-nonsense but fun dialogue Jess has with her recipes is fresh and different from other books.

I put down my galley (remember, the real book was not yet printed when I wrote this), knowing that SALADS ARE GOOD; SALADS ARE HEALTHY; SALADS NEVER HAVE TO BE BORING; AND THAT DRESSINGS CAN ALWAYS BE HOME-MADE—NEVER, EVER OUT OF A JAR!

I chose five salads right off the bat to make over the next five days: Spring Lettuces, Avocado, and Creamy Dressing (page 112); Martha's Mango and Mozzarella with Young Lettuces (page 114); the BLT Potato Salad (page 150); Cantaloupe, Cucumbers, Lime, and Mint (page 180); and Watermelon, Shiso, Plum, and Salt (page 184).

I am on my way to nicknaming myself a "salad freak."

well, hello

The title *Salad Freak* started as a joke. While I wrestled with imagining the book on my shelf and couldn't, and lost sleep over whether I was ready to become "the salad freak," it became more and more painfully obvious that I already was.

I am truly obsessed with making salads. Salads have always been my favorite thing to prepare and the dish I look forward to eating the most. Wandering the farmers' market for inspiration, tears building behind my eyes because of the sheer beauty of the gentle blush and deep purple hues of the fleeting winter chicories, gasping at the first sight of bright Sungold tomatoes and remem-

bering their sweetness, eating an entire paper bag full of fresh peas before I get home—that all makes sense to me. Sure, I went to the French Culinary Institute and learned to use butter, bacon, and sugar for flavor. Sure, I can appreciate a fresh truffle grated on a decadent pasta—but I've always been interested in making food that felt fresh, or as I like to call it, "taking the raw off."

If this has become a safe space to talk about my obsessions, it would be the time to talk about Martha Stewart. While I never "did my time" in restaurants and some may say that affects my credibility as a chef, those people have not been cooking for Martha for over ten years. I have worked with Martha in many different capacities, but one of my favorites has always been making meals for her, especially lunch. It has been during my "Martha Years" that I have been able to really refine my salad making. The lunches I would prepare for Martha became known as my "three-hour salads." This involved going to the farmers' market for the best possible ingredients available that day and then preparing each component with more focus and attention than I even knew I had in me. Sometimes she would give me a prompt like, "I'm in the mood for something light and fresh and truly delicious," or she would bring in pastel-hued eggs from her chickens with the deepest orange yolks I've ever seen. My whole morning would be sorting the perfect crunchy inner leaves from a head of butter lettuce, toasting nuts to that just-right golden brown, and creating unique vinaigrettes every day that gave just the right amount of pinch in the cheeks but were bright or creamy, depending on what would complement but not overpower the other ingredients.

Making salads became something of its own art form for me. A channel for my perfectionist tendencies, an outlet for creative expression. Every dish I made was sort of a salad. As my career began to focus more on food styling, I began to consider the visual composition just as much as the culinary one and making salads became even more fun. A salad has everything going for it—a careful (but playful) balance of flavors, textures, shapes, and colors. Just as much as I love making salads, I love sharing them too, and showing you how easy it can be to make a really mind-blowing and exceptionally beautiful salad.

Whether you're already a self-proclaimed salad freak, you're working on becoming one, or you're just trying to eat a little cleaner, I hope this book will give you a lot of inspiration, and teach you techniques that will build confidence and help you make better (and anything but boring) salads you'll want to eat every day.

light,
fresh, and
truly
delicious,
or about
this book

A salad can be a side dish, but it shouldn't get stuck being an afterthought. A spread of seasonal salads can make the most beautiful, colorful, and delicious dinner party table that will leave all your guests dreaming of the flavors they enjoyed. I eat salads first thing in the morning too—whether it's a big bowl of citrus or thick, juicy slices of tomato— why not?

In this book, you'll find recipes for salads for breakfast, lunch, and dinner; and salads that are hearty enough for a main course, and others that are light, fresh partners to pair with anything else you feel like making. There is a pizza piled high with salad, a really simple egg salad, vegan salads, and even a gazpacho. There are salads your kids might eat, and salads that are almost too pretty to eat. Most are quick to assemble, and should be served immediately after making them while the flavors are fresh and textures crisp, but the few more involved recipes are worth it for a special occasion.

These are salads that are inspired by certain ingredients, colors, flavors, and places. Chapters are split up into seasons, to remind us to take a moment to enjoy the best produce at its peak. It just tastes better that way, and you'll notice the difference it makes immediately. Ingredients in the recipes are organized by fresh produce, dairy, meat, and pantry items to make it easier to organize what you'll need to shop for and what you might already have on hand. There is a separate dressings index (page 255) for when you are ready to riff on your own.

I share food styling tips whenever I can to help you make your dishes look like they do in the photos. I've considered shapes and colors and the composition of the dish and when it's important to the look, texture, or flavor of the dish, I'll give detailed instructions for preparing the ingredients— I won't assume that you'll know when to use a mandoline to get perfect carrot ribbons or soak radishes in ice water to crisp them up. Sometimes these details might seem a bit fussy, but with a little practice they will start to become second nature and good habits in the kitchen.

We are all looking for ways to eat more healthfully without feeling restricted. And with creative approaches, salads offer endless variety. This isn't a diet cookbook, but it is a guide to eating in a vegetable-forward way without ever getting bored. I've made all 100 salads in this book, many times, and I'm still not sick of them (really!).

It took me a long time to just lean into looking at what I love doing as a form of mindfulness.

A quick glance at my bookshelf reveals an almost obsessive interest in self-improvement, spirituality, mindfulness, and meditation. In my intense search for finding the thing that was going to work for me, I found myself fixated on everything I wasn't doing yet—I was trying too hard.

It's easy to get lost in making a salad if you let yourself. The prep of washing and sorting lettuce leaves is about as meditative as it gets. Unfortunately, a lot of food media today doesn't focus on the benefits of spending time preparing good food; it's all about hacks, shortcuts, and how to get something onto the table with as little effort as possible.

My salads aren't difficult or time-consuming, but they are designed to be made with intention. What I'm suggesting here isn't exactly salads as self-care, but also, it is. I'm not saying you'll have a spiritual experience, but I do hope you'll be able to focus on each task and let the weight of the day and any other little things in your mind go.

Take a deep breath before you start chopping. Take another look at the spectacular colorful veins of that Swiss chard before you tear it apart. More than anything, acknowledge that you're making an effort for yourself and maybe someone else and feel good about that.

a note on mindfulness

pantry

My pantry doesn't look like it belongs in a magazine, or even in this book. It's messy, and cluttered, and overcrowded because I love trying new ingredients. I carry a separate suitcase when I travel just to bring back ingredients I find, and then I hoard them. But, no matter how many new things I try, I find myself going back to the same ingredients over and over again. If you have most of these items, you'll be well prepared to make a vast array of salads without having to run out and grab anything other than the fresh stuff.

VINEGARS

I bought a stand-alone pantry to fit all my vinegars in instead of just keeping the ones I really need. You don't need to do that (you just need a few), but if you love making salads, you should start to build your collection and keep all of these vinegars on hand. I do think it's worth it to spurge on exceptional quality ones sometimes, and they do last quite a while. This is in alphabetical order, not preference.

APPLE CIDER: Bragg's is the best, in my opinion. Pineapple Collaborative also makes a very fancy one in a beautiful bottle that will look nice on your counter.

BALSAMIC: It is worth getting a good one if you love balsamic vinegar, and be careful not to mistake balsamic vinegar for balsamic glaze. They are not the same thing! Balsamic glaze is a syrup and should not be used in salads, or maybe, period. I like the O Olive Oil & Vinegar company's fig balsamic because it has a unique sweetness, or anything from Modena.

CHAMPAGNE: I prefer this to white wine vinegar (which I never use, apparently). It is brighter and a bit sweeter. I like the one by O Olive Oil & Vinegar.

RED WINE: I think this one is really worth splurging on. Someone gave me a fancy bottle of Camino red wine vinegar and it ruined me.

RICE (UNSEASONED): Marukan and Kikkoman are available in every grocery store and are just fine, but I sometimes grab a nicer bottle if I'm already at the Japanese supermarket. I also really love brown rice vinegar, which you can buy at the Japanese market as well. It's a little toastier and has a bit more flavor. I also like to keep O Olive Oil & Vinegar yuzu rice vinegar on hand.

SHERRY: I usually buy Columela because it's the best option at the grocery store. Don't buy the cheapest one, but it should only be somewhere around $10. Keepwell Vinegar and O Olive Oil & Vinegar have options in this price range that are great.

WHITE BALSAMIC: I absolutely love white balsamic vinegar. It's my favorite vinegar, and I use it constantly. I love its sweetness. I love its tartness. I love it combined with lemon. Sometimes it's called white balsamic condiment or white vinegar condiment at Italian specialty stores. O Olive Oil & Vinegar makes my favorite.

WHITE VINEGAR: I keep a bulk-size jug of Heinz white vinegar around because it's good for a lot of things, especially cleaning your sink.

OILS

EXTRA-VIRGIN OLIVE OIL: I keep two olive oils on hand—one for cooking and making most vinaigrettes, and one bottle for drizzling. California Olive Ranch 100% California is my go-to olive oil for almost everything, and they offer other varieties at different price points, including a high-quality drizzling oil. For finishing, I love Pineapple Collaborative's oil; it's bright and citrusy, it's produced by women, and it's basically liquid gold. Wonder Valley is another fancier favorite that is extremely bold, made by wonderful people in California.

AVOCADO: Avocado has become my go-to neutral oil for vinaigrettes. It has virtually no flavor and is better for you than canola oil. Avocado oil goes rancid fairly fast, so don't buy this one in bulk. Stick to small bottles and store it in a cool, dark place.

ROASTED PUMPKIN SEED OIL: Pumpkin seed oil is delicious, unique, and really worth trying. It is sweet and as thick as motor oil and feels super decadent when drizzled on anything from sweet potatoes to vanilla ice cream.

OIL FOR DEEP-FRYING: You'll need to keep oil around for the frying in this book. I usually use SAFFLOWER or SUNFLOWER oil for frying over CANOLA oil, but these are three options with neutral flavor and a high smoke point. PEANUT oil is another good option if no one has a peanut allergy.

TOASTED WALNUT OIL: I love walnut oil. It's fragrant and toasty and adds a subtle je ne sais quoi to dressings; it's especially nice on salads with nutty cheese.

TOASTED SESAME OIL: Use this as a finishing oil or to flavor vinaigrettes. A little goes a long way. I store mine in the fridge because it can go rancid fairy quickly.

MUSTARDS

WHOLE GRAIN: Maille grainy mustard is what I use 98 percent of the time when making vinaigrettes. It is simply the best. If you want to be really fancy, Pommery is also very good. I love tang and the little pop that mustard seeds give to vinaigrettes.

DIJON: Maille or Grey Poupon Dijon.

SALTS

KOSHER SALT: I use Diamond Crystal kosher salt and I think it's important you seek this out. It's the perfect salt for everyday cooking. If you can't find Diamond Crystal, Morton's or David's kosher salt are other options with slightly different crystal size (they will be a little saltier and slower to dissolve).

FLAKY SALT: Maldon is the best, I think, but feel free to use whatever you want to get that little extra crunch.

OTHER CONDIMENTS, OR THINGS THAT COME IN A JAR OR CAN

ANCHOVIES: Anchovies add that umami flavor that people go crazy for—even those that claim to not like anchovies. I buy them in a jar because the tins are messy.

CAPERS: If they are salt-packed instead of bottled in brine, you'll need to rinse before you use them, but I don't have a preference between those and the ones bottled in brine!

FISH SAUCE: Red Boat fish sauce is the best; a little goes a long way!

HONEY: I always like to buy something local if I can, and raw is even better.

MAYONNAISE: PLEASE, ONLY USE HELLMANN'S OR BEST FOODS MAYONNAISE. THE ONLY EXCEPTION IS WHEN I CALL FOR KEWPIE JAPANESE MAYONNAISE. BUT PLEASE, PLEASE, USE ONE OF THESE OR NOTHING WILL TASTE LIKE IT IS SUPPOSED TO TASTE.

MAPLE SYRUP: I went to college in Vermont, so I truly believe Vermont syrup is the best thing and there should be no exceptions for real, pure, high-quality maple syrup. It's a wonderful sweetener for dressings and just a hint will transform roasted vegetables.

MISO: White miso is best for vinaigrettes and roasting vegetables (or adding to soups)! Mild and a little funky, it adds a really rich umami flavor.

OLIVES: I keep a variety on hand, not just for salad making but for serving as a snack when guests come over (try warming them up in a little olive oil with some fennel seeds and chile). I love big, buttery green olives the most (like Castelvetrano and Cerignola), but also like to have some Kalamata, Niçoise, and oil-cured black Moroccan olives on hand at all times too.

POMEGRANATE MOLASSES: Pomegranate juice that has been reduced down to tangy, sweet syrup makes a really bright and special vinaigrette. It can also be used as a sweetener or glaze, or just drizzled over roasted vegetables or dips.

SOY SAUCE: I use tamari because it's gluten-free, a bit richer in flavor, and a little less salty than regular soy sauce.

SUGAR: I like to use natural cane sugar for everything because it has slightly more flavor and feels like it's better for me, even though it's still just sugar. I also keep light and dark brown sugar on hand.

TAHINI: I only use tahini on one salad in this book, which is crazy, because I love it. Tahini and lemon dressing is one you could put on anything, really.

TUNA IN A JAR: When you are making a salad, you really want to use the best-quality tuna you can, and this usually comes packed in olive oil in a jar. It's more expensive, but it's really, really good—and you're not mixing this with mayonnaise and putting this on a sandwich, so trust me, it's worth it, and it is often on sale.

YUZU KOSHO: This wonderful Japanese condiment is a really bright, refreshing way to add a bit of heat.

BEANS

I buy dried beans and canned beans. There is no question that dried beans taste better, but I never have the foresight to soak them in advance. I love how quickly canned beans can make a last-minute meal come together.

BLACK BEANS
BUTTER BEANS
CANNELLINI BEANS
CHICKPEAS
GREAT NORTHERN BEANS
LENTILS

GRAINS

Grains are a great way to make a salad feel more substantial, and add different textures and a bit of nuttiness. Grain flours are also essential pantry ingredients. These are some of my favorites that I've used in this book.

ALL-PURPOSE FLOUR

BLACK RICE

BREADCRUMBS

BROWN RICE (SHORT GRAIN)

FARRO (NOT QUICK COOKING)

OLD-FASHIONED ROLLED OATS

PANKO BREADCRUMBS

PUFFED RICE CEREAL

QUINOA

RICE FLOUR

RICE NOODLES

SOBA NOODLES

TOASTED BUCKWHEAT GROATS (KASHA)

WILD RICE

SEEDS AND NUTS

Nuts should always be toasted. Set your oven to 425°F (220°C) and toast until golden and fragrant, 6 to 10 minutes. Make sure you set a timer. No one ever remembers to check on their nuts until they are already burning; it's just a fact.

ALMONDS: Whole raw, sliced, and smoked (when sliced, toast them a bit more quickly).

CASHEWS

CHIA SEEDS

FLAX SEEDS

HAZELNUTS: I prefer skin on.

HEMP SEEDS

PEANUTS: I prefer roasted, salted, and skin on.

PECANS

PEPITAS

PINE NUTS: Avoid cheaper pine nuts that can leave a metallic taste in your mouth. Try to find pine nuts that were grown in California or the Mediterranean.

PISTACHIOS: Santa Barbara Pistachio Company produces the best pistachios; order them online in bulk! They're so worth it. Sicilian pistachios from Bronte are also very, very special (and very, very expensive).

POPPY SEEDS

SUNFLOWER SEEDS

WALNUTS

WHITE SESAME SEEDS: I buy them pre-toasted!

SPICES

Where you buy your spices from really matters. Grocery store spices tend to be really old and stale. Try ordering them online from Burlap & Barrel, Diaspora Co., or New York Shuk, where they may be a little pricey, but are single-origin, super high-quality, and responsibly sourced, or reputable spice stores like Kalustyan's or SOS Chefs. And don't buy spices in bulk unless you're really blowing through them! Make sure they are sealed tightly and kept in a cool, dark place, and remember, they don't last forever. My grandmother still had spices from the '60s in her cabinets in the '90s. I have wondered for decades if that was why all of her food was so bland.

ALEPPO PEPPER

ANCHO CHILE POWDER

BLACK GARLIC

BLACK PEPPERCORNS

CALABRIAN CHILE: Whole or crushed.

CINNAMON

CORIANDER SEEDS

CRUSHED RED PEPPER

CUMIN SEEDS

FENNEL SEEDS
GARLIC POWDER
SAFFRON
SMOKED PAPRIKA
SUMAC
TURMERIC
ZA'ATAR (see page 262)

DRIED FRUITS

We've come a long way from Craisins. Dried fruit adds a beautiful sweetness to salads and to vinaigrettes.
DATES
FIGS
GOLDEN RAISINS
THOMPSON RAISINS

fridge

Citrus and fresh herbs are the heart and soul of every dish I make. Get in the habit of stocking up when you go shopping.

CITRUS

I always keep my refrigerator stocked with lemons, limes, and a variety of oranges. They look beautiful out on the counter in a bowl, but they will go bad quickly. I'm pretty sure I use at least one of these things in every recipe, so I just make it a habit to add to the list any time I go out shopping.

FRESH HERBS

I pick up bunches of parsley, cilantro, mint, and scallions every time I go shopping—they add something fresh and a lot of flavor. Dill, basil, and chives don't get used as often, but you also must buy these fresh. Herbs are a great thing to try to grow at home, even if it's just on a windowsill—so you can just clip what you need! See tips for storing on page 27.

DAIRY

A little bit of dairy in a salad can go a long way—contributing salt, tang, umami, and richness, as well as a variety of textures.
BLUE CHEESE
BUTTERMILK
CHEDDAR
EGGS
FETA (I like Valbreso or French; it's creamier)
FRESH BURRATA
GOAT CHEESE
GOUDA
HOMEMADE RICOTTA (page 259)
LABNEH
MOZZARELLA
PARMESAN
PECORINO
YOGURT

setting yourself up for salad success

If you're reading this, you probably already have at least a knife. But who knows! Having the right tools for the job makes life much easier, and doesn't take up too much drawer space, I promise. These are the essential tools for making salads, and a few that you don't absolutely need, but might like to have around.

SALAD SPINNER: Say hello to your new best friend. Get yourself a good, big one, like the one from OXO. Why is this the first thing on my list? You will be washing a lot of lettuce. The salad spinner helps make this as quick and efficient as it can be. Gentle spinning sends water shooting off of leaves, keeping fragile leaves intact. Vinaigrettes just won't stick to wet leaves.

MIXING BOWLS: You're going to need some mixing bowls. A solid set of stainless-steel bowls of various sizes should be plenty for dressing, tossing, whatever you need to do.

CHEF'S AND/OR SANTOKU KNIFE: Get yourself a good knife. You don't need to buy a whole expensive block. Buy something made of German steel and it will be easy to sharpen and will last forever. I have very fancy Japanese knives, but I use my Wüsthof and Henkels knives every day for their weight and ease. I think santoku knives really make it easier to slice, dice, and chop—and are very helpful while you're still working on your knife skills.

PARING KNIFE: I love Kuhn Rikon ceramic or Victorinox paring knives with plastic handles. If I buy an expensive paring knife, it gets beat up in my drawer, or I lose it or chip it. Maybe that's just me, but these have always worked well.

OFFSET SERRATED KNIFE: The Wüsthof deli knife or the Dexter offset bread knife might not seem like a salad-making essential, but just wait until you start chopping nuts with one of these.

JAPANESE MANDOLINE: I use my Benriner mandoline every day. I occasionally shave off a piece of my thumb, which everyone will do at some point—just try to pay attention when you're using it. Don't get overconfident, don't move too fast, and replace it when the blade starts to dull. I know it seems scary, but once you get used it, it will make your salads super elegant—no one can slice that thinly and evenly on their own.

MICROPLANE: The Microplane is my desert island kitchen tool. Citrus zest is truly my secret weapon and adds the brightness I constantly crave in my cooking. Don't try to use anything else; you need a rasp grater in your life. Also great for grating ginger, and to create fluffy clouds of finely grated cheese.

CITRUS SQUEEZER: There are a lot of different kinds of citrus juicers and reamers, but Martha swears you get the most juice from a Mexican-style hand juicer.

REUSABLE PRODUCE STORAGE: Reusable produce storage items not only cut down on food waste and plastic waste, but they have been created to help produce last longer. I love OXO's produce keeper for herbs, and reusable bags that you moisten with water like linen bags by Ambrosia or cotton bags by Well Earth for lettuces and other greens. I have no idea how they work, but the Debbie Meyer reusable green bags sold in grocery stores also really help keep produce fresh.

A GOOD PEPPER MILL: My whole childhood I grew up with cursed pepper grinders that never worked, and no one loves black pepper more than my dad. It's hard to go wrong with a Peugeot U'Select pepper grinder or an Atlas brass or chrome pepper mill. Freshly ground pepper makes a big difference in any cooking, but especially in vinaigrettes and over the top of salads.

A PLATING SPOON: This is where the list may seem to get excessive, but I ask you to swoop and swirl many things in this book. Yes, you can do it with a regular spoon—but I absolutely love my Ruhlman spoon that was made just for creating the perfect swoop of sauce on a plate.

GREENS STRIPPER: I didn't think I needed this either, but if you're eating kale even half as much as I do, this will save you time, and also stop you from wasting greens like I used to be very guilty of.

JOYCE CHEN SCISSORS: Whether you're cutting lettuces and herbs from your garden or not, these scissors will come in handy. Their sharp precision tip and big loopy handles make them easy to use for perfect snips (from trimming carrot tops to making floral arrangements).

Y-PEELER: Kuhn Rikon Swiss Y-peelers are another tool I use every single day. It may take a bit of getting used to if you've only had a traditional potato peeler, but you can peel anything with these things.

JULIENNE PEELER: Now, you could do this by hand, and technically your mandoline can do this . . . and it feels like I'm giving away a hard-earned food stylist secret, but the OXO julienne peeler makes the most beautiful long, even, and slightly curved julienned vegetables.

HALF AND QUARTER SHEET PANS: I suggest having a few of each size and buying a quality brand like Nordic Ware that isn't flimsy and will last quite a while. They can discolor if you put them in the dishwasher, which doesn't affect how they work—but Martha washes them by hand, so I do too.

questions to ask yourself when shopping for salads

IS IT IN SEASON?

The easiest way to make sure is by shopping at your local farmers' market, signing up for a CSA or other delivery service, or growing your own vegetables—which doesn't have to be expensive. If none of these sounds reasonable, do a quick search to find out what is in season where and think twice before reaching for a watermelon or tomatoes in December. Produce is meant to be enjoyed at its peak—and all of these salads were created with that in mind. Wherever you're shopping, if you stick to what is in season, it's going to taste better—so use the chapters of this book as a guide and you won't be disappointed.

WHEN TO BUY ORGANIC?

PRODUCE: Any produce that has a skin that you will be eating: apples, blueberries, celery, cherries, cucumbers, grapes, herbs (fresh), kale, lemons, lettuce, limes, nectarines, peaches, pears, peppers, potatoes, strawberries, tomatoes.

NUTS AND SEEDS

MEAT AND DAIRY: Look for cage-free and hormone- and antibiotic-free eggs, humanely raised meat and poultry, and milk and yogurt.

WHEN TO SPLURGE?

BUTTER: I like to keep a more expensive European-style or cultured butter on hand for salads. I only use a little bit, and better butter makes it a lot richer and more special.

OLIVE OIL: See page 18.

SALT AND PEPPER: See pages 18 and 23.

PARMESAN AND PECORINO CHEESE: Always go for the good stuff with a rind. It's worth it.

HONEY AND MAPLE SYRUP: Only the real stuff will do!

IS IT RIPE?

SMELL IT!: Peaches, pineapples, and cantaloupe and honeydew melons should be fragrant if they are ready to eat.

SQUEEZE IT!: Avocados, mangoes, peaches, pears, and tomatoes should all be tender to the touch.

TAP IT!: Watermelons should have a good hollow sound when tapped.

Washing and drying greens properly is the most important part of making a salad. There is nothing worse than preparing a salad, taking the first bite, and discovering it's gritty or sandy. Drying is also essential—vinaigrettes just won't stick to damp leaves.

My advice, as someone who has lost their fair share of beautiful greens to the back of the fridge, is to get into the habit of washing and storing all of your lettuces and herbs as soon as you get home from the market while you're putting away your groceries. Prepped lettuce that is ready to grab and use is always going to get used, and when it's stored properly, it will stay fresh a lot longer.

The recipes in this book assume that all bagged greens have been carefully washed and dried. See below for a few tips on prepping your greens.

USING A SALAD SPINNER: Fill the salad spinner with very cold water (even throw a few ice cubes in it—cold water will help perk up any limp greens). Place the greens in the basket, tearing the leaves into bite-size pieces and sorting out any brown or damaged pieces. Put your hand in the water with your fingers separated and move them around for about 30 seconds—gently, as to not damage the leaves, but agitating the water enough to knock off any dirt or sand that is stuck on the leaves. Let the leaves sit in the water for a few minutes as the sediment sinks to the bottom.

Remove the basket—if the water is really dirty, I recommend repeating this process. Then empty the bowl of water, rinsing it if necessary, replace the basket, and spin dry. Sometimes I have to empty the bowl out, then spin again.

HEADS OF LETTUCE: Trim off the end, separate into leaves, and wash and dry in a salad spinner. Tear leaves into bite-size pieces, if large. Store in a reusable produce bag misted with a bit of water every couple of days, or wrap in damp paper towels and store in a sealed plastic bag.

LOOSE LEAVES: These are usually prewashed even when you're buying at the farmers' market, but one quick dunk and spin in the salad spinner is a good idea. Store in a reusable produce bag misted with water every couple of days, or wrap in damp paper towels in a sealed plastic bag. I like to use my OXO produce keeper for particularly delicate or tender greens.

TENDER HERBS: Parsley, cilantro, and mint should be washed in a salad spinner, spun dry, and stored in a reusable produce bag misted with a bit of water every couple of days, or kept in an OXO produce keeper (this keeps them from getting squished), or loosely wrapped in damp paper towels and sealed in a plastic bag. I snip the ends of my basil and put it in a glass of water like a bouquet of flowers, cover it with a plastic bag to keep it humid, and keep it at room temperature, changing out the water every day.

music to make salads by

I remember my grandfather singing along to Pavarotti in broken Italian while making meatballs just as well as I remember the smell of frying onions and garlic that wafted through that small kitchen with fluorescent lights tinged yellow and ochre linoleum floors. And there was me bopping around to Cat Stevens arranging Cheddar-and-Triscuit platters, looking out onto the shallow sparkling fingers of Crab Creek at my childhood friend Maggie's house, in a gorgeous kitchen with counter space for miles. Laughing and moving in place with my friend Lauryn, listening to Italo disco while making a huge pot of pasta sauce getting ready to feed thirty of our friends. Brooklyn has its own harsh symphony of horns and screeches to wake you up, but now, settled in Los Angeles, there is a constant parade of synthesizer bleeps and bloops carrying me with heavy eyelids through the morning. When every day is sunny and in the seventies, a long, slow breakfast with my partner, Ben, can somehow be drawn out to the afternoon.

The part of your brain that creates and processes sound must be the same part of your brain that inspires cooking and appreciating taste and smells. Maybe it's just the creation of a mood, an energy. I'm not a scientist, and maybe it's just how my mind works, but I do know that music in the kitchen is something that is absolutely imperative for me. Everyone has a different kind of music that feels right to them and puts them at ease, and the wrong kind of music can really make you crazy. Some jazz, for example, scrambles my brain. I don't know if it's the unrelenting brush on the high hats or the manic and unpredictable zooming clarinet, but I can't think straight. I love singing along to music while I'm cooking, but I also love listening to songs in different languages so I'm not focusing on the words.

I encourage you to experiment, and find what works for you. Think about what you need in that moment: Are you tired; do you need something that will give you a little energy? Are you buzzing and need something to put you at ease? Are you tight? Need to get loose? Do you love singing along to songs you know by heart? I've thought long and hard about a few albums that I think are a good place to start. I can't guarantee there is something for everyone, but I've made an honest attempt.

This will take you to my Spotify account, where I've been making a playlist every month for a long time.

Here are a few of my favorite albums to listen to while cooking:

ALICE COLTRANE,
Journey in Satchidananda

BEACH BOYS,
Pet Sounds

BEVERLY GLENN-COPELAND,
Keyboard Fantasies

DAN DEACON,
Gliss Riffer

DOMENIQUE DUMONT,
People on Sunday

FOOLS,
Fools' Harp, Vol. 1

FRANCIS BEBEY,
Psychedelic Sanza 1982–1984

GREEN-HOUSE,
Six Songs for Invisible Gardens

HAMA,
Houmeissa

HANS-JOACHIM ROEDELIUS,
Wenn der Südwind Weht

HARALD GROSSKOPF,
Synthesist

HARUOMI HOSONO,
Paraiso

HIROSHI YOSHIMURA,
Green

JOHN CARROLL KIRBY,
Tuscany and *Septet*

JOHN MOODS,
The Essential John Moods

JON HASSELL
Vernal Equinox (remastered)

JONI MITCHELL,
Hejira

THE MAMA'S AND THE PAPA'S,
If You Can Believe Your Eyes & Ears

MAMMAN SANI ABDOULAYE,
Unreleased Tapes 1981–1984

MULATU ASTATKE,
Éthiopiques, Vol. 4, Ethio Jazz & Musique Instrumentale, 1969–1974

ORCHESTRE POLY-RYTHMO DE COTONOU,
Echos Hypnotiques, Vol. 2

PATRICK COWLEY,
Afternooners

PAUL MCCARTNEY AND LINDA MCCARTNEY,
Ram

PECKER,
Pecker Power

PETER IVERS,
Becoming Peter Ivers

PHILIP GLASS,
Glassworks

PIPER,
Summer Breeze

QUARTETO EM CY,
Quarteto em Cy

ROBERTA FLACK,
First Take

SUZANNE CIANI,
Seven Waves

there are few things on earth that make me feel the way i feel when i look at a chicory. i would like to say more, but what else is there to say?

Winter in New York can be a very dark time. The days are short, and I spend most of them inside to avoid the harsh cold. Winter in New York is something I complain about multiple times a day. I always try to escape. The gray skies, the dirty snow, it all makes me long for sun and brightness.

Some people, in their desire for warmth and comfort, crave heavy foods—macaroni and cheese, slow-cooked stews and braises, brown foods that stick to your ribs. But I make sure I have a romantic partner and debate whether or not I need to buy a SAD lamp. I read too many self-help books and eat three Sumo mandarins a day. I order citrus in bulk and venture from Brooklyn into Manhattan just to get the pink chicory. The winter is a dark time, but it is also when some of the brightest food and my favorite flavors are in season.

new year's eve citrus, avocado, and little radish salad

(THIS PAIRS WELL WITH ALMOST ANYTHING.)   SERVES 6 TO 8 AS A STARTER

I have found it hard to make holiday traditions that stick, but this is a salad that has stuck with me. It will always remind me of my first winter in California, the ceaseless joy I get from bringing home a bounty of citrus from the farmers' market, and the Paul McCartney song "Monkberry Moon Delight." New Year's can be a loaded holiday, but this is the food embodiment of the "in with the new" sentiment. And it's pretty.

PRODUCE

3 to 4 mixed citrus, such as Oro Blanco and pink grapefruit, Cara Cara oranges, blood oranges

2 handfuls baby radishes, or 1 bunch small radishes

3 perfectly ripe avocados

PANTRY

Good extra-virgin olive oil

Flaky salt

PREP: First things first, take a look at the Styling Tip, opposite, on how to supreme citrus. If you'll be supreming ahead of time, store the segments in their own juice. If you're using a mix, I usually keep my blood oranges separate so they don't stain the other more lightly colored fruits.

Prepare an ice bath. If you're using small radishes, thinly slice 1 bunch on a mandoline— leaving any tiny good-looking tender greens attached if you can—and add them to the ice bath as you go. (You shouldn't need to do this with the baby radishes, but it does help perk up any limp greens.) Soak radishes for about 10 minutes to crisp up. Pat dry on a clean kitchen towel or paper towels.

Halve, pit, peel, and slice 3 avocados.

ASSEMBLE AND SERVE: Layer the avocados and citrus, then sprinkle the radishes on top of everything. Drizzle a little of the reserved citrus juice over everything—just a little, you don't want a puddle. The acidic juices will help to keep the avocados from oxidizing. Drizzle with a bit of your best olive oil and sprinkle with flaky salt.

STYLING TIP

Use a sharp knife to slice the ends off the fruit, exposing the flesh. Stand the fruit on a flat end. With the knife, working your way from the top to the bottom, remove the rind and pith but as little of the flesh as possible.

Hold the fruit in your hand. With a paring knife, carefully slice on both sides of the segment between the membranes to free the supreme.

Let the supremes drop into a bowl and, if storing, squeeze the remaining juice over the bowl. You can keep the supremes covered with plastic wrap or in a sealed container in the fridge for a day, but I don't recommend more than that as they will start to get a bit bitter.

citrus breakfast salad with spicy chile granola

SERVES 2 TO 4 AS A BREAKFAST, WITH ABOUT 4 CUPS (400 G) GRANOLA LEFT OVER

I made this salad for the first time in the woods of the Russian River Valley and ate it on a porch overlooking the trees while wearing a bathrobe. I isolated myself in an A-frame cabin for five days to write, but first loaded up on ingredients at the farmers' market in San Francisco. I made it with avocados, and you can do that too. If you want to save time, you can use store-bought artisanal granola here.

PRODUCE

4 to 6 of your favorite mixed citrus, such as blood oranges, Cara Cara oranges, grapefruit, and Satsuma mandarins

DAIRY

2 egg whites, beaten

Sheep's milk yogurt (plain or maple flavored), for serving (optional)

PANTRY

⅓ cup (75 ml) extra-virgin olive oil

3 tablespoons crushed red pepper flakes (I like the brightness of Calabrian chiles)

1 teaspoon ground cinnamon

3 cups (265 g) old-fashioned oats (not quick cooking)

½ cup (85 g) toasted buckwheat groats (kasha)

½ cup (about 75 g) seeds (flax, hemp, sesame—go crazy)

½ cup (50 g) sliced almonds

½ cup (120 ml) good maple syrup (only the best will do, seriously)

2 teaspoons kosher salt

Flaky salt

PREP: Preheat the oven to 350°F (175°C).

Slice and segment the citrus (see Styling Tip, opposite).

COOK: In a small pot over medium heat, bring ⅓ cup (75 ml) olive oil and 3 tablespoons red pepper flakes to a simmer and then remove from the heat. Swirl in 1 teaspoon cinnamon and let sit for a few minutes (the longer it sits, the spicier it will be; I like to let it cool to room temperature). Strain into a large bowl though a fine-mesh sieve; remove 1 tablespoon or so of the spicy oil and set aside for drizzling later.

To that same large bowl with the spicy oil, add 3 cups (265 g) oats, ½ cup (85 g) buckwheat, ½ cup (about 75 g) seeds, ½ cup (50 g) almonds, ½ cup (120 ml) maple syrup, 2 teaspoons kosher salt, and 2 egg whites. Combine with a wooden spoon or your hands until everything is mixed and moistened.

Transfer to a parchment-lined rimmed baking sheet and bake, rotating and mixing every 15 minutes, until golden brown and fragrant, 25 to 30 minutes.

ASSEMBLE AND SERVE: Arrange the citrus on your plate or plates. Scatter with a handful of granola and top with a spoonful of yogurt (use the back of your spoon to give it a nice swoop), if desired. Drizzle with the reserved spicy oil and sprinkle with flaky salt. Save any remaining granola in an airtight container for up to 3 weeks.

STYLING TIP

Any time I'm using a variety of citrus I try to prepare each differently for visual appeal. Using a sharp knife, I remove the pith and peel from larger oranges such as navel, blood, or Cara Cara and slice some into rounds and others into supremes (see page 37). For tangerines and mandarins, I peel them and separate the segments to scatter on top.

mandarins and cream

As a kid, the appeal of the combination of vanilla and orange juice in the Orange Julius eluded me. Maybe it's because I didn't grow up in Southern California. But now I'm making up for lost time, constantly finding excuses to pair tangy oranges with smooth sweet cream. In this salad, I love using mandarins because they have a really special brightness—Sumo mandarins in particular taste almost like orange Gatorade or soda. This makes a perfect breakfast or dessert and works really well with the Homemade Ricotta on page 259.

PREP: Peel 1 Sumo, 2 Satsuma, and 2 Kishu (or any other available variety) mandarins and separate the segments.

ASSEMBLE AND SERVE: Place 4 to 6 ounces (115 to 170 g) burrata on a plate and scatter the mandarin segments around and on top of it. Drizzle with your best olive oil and sprinkle with salt.

PRODUCE
1 Sumo mandarin

2 Satsuma mandarins

2 Kishu, Pixie, or other small mandarins or clementines

DAIRY
4 to 6 ounces (115 to 170 g) fresh burrata

PANTRY
Good extra-virgin olive oil, something bright and citrusy

Flaky salt

40

a few of my favorite things

SERVES 2 TO 4 AS A LIGHT LUNCH OR SERVE WITH GRILLED CHICKEN OR SKIRT STEAK

This salad is bright, tangy, crunchy, and salty, all of my favorite things. It also features Oro Blanco, or white grapefruit, which is bright, tart, and less bitter than regular grapefruit, and my favorite flavor. The absolute most delicious pistachios come from the Santa Barbara Pistachio Company, and you'll think I'm crazy, but I suggest you order them or buy them because it will change your life—or at least this salad.

PRODUCE

4 baby beets (about 8 ounces/225 g; a mix of colors here is nice but not necessary)

4 smallish, thin carrots (about 8 ounces/225 g)

2 Oro Blanco grapefruit, or any variety you can find

1 handful fresh mint leaves

DAIRY

4 ounces (115 g) French or Bulgarian feta cheese

PANTRY

1 cup (240 ml) rice vinegar

¼ cup (50 g) sugar

1 teaspoon kosher salt

Extra-virgin olive oil

Flaky salt

1 handful shelled pistachios, toasted (see page 20) and chopped

PREP: Peel 4 baby beets and slice them very thin, preferably on a mandoline (tip: wear gloves if you don't want to stain your hands). Put the slices in a small bowl or jar, and separate by color, if you are using different colored beets.

In a small saucepan, bring to a boil 1 cup (240 ml) rice vinegar, ¼ cup (50 g) sugar, and 1 teaspoon salt. Pour the liquid over the beets and let them cool completely (you can do this a few days in advance and store in the refrigerator).

Carefully slice 4 carrots on a mandoline, lengthwise. If your carrots have a little green on them, leave it. Really watch your fingers here, and use the guard for your mandoline. Shave the entire length of the carrot. If you don't have a mandoline, or feel too nervous, use a Y-peeler. Put the shaved carrots in ice-cold water until they are ready to use; this will make them stiffen up and get curly.

Supreme 2 grapefruit over a bowl, and squeeze the grapefruit guts over the segments into the bowl. See the detailed instructions for supreming on page 37 and the Styling Tip on page 39.

ASSEMBLE AND SERVE: Thinly slice 4 ounces (115 g) feta, and use that as a base to build the salad on. Add layers of the grapefruit segments, pickled beets, and shaved carrots. Drizzle some of the grapefruit juice over the salad, drizzle with oil, and sprinkle with flaky salt. Tuck 1 handful mint leaves throughout and scatter with 1 handful toasted pistachios.

crispy chicken with gingery cabbage, mandarins, and almonds

SERVES 2 AS A MAIN DISH

I don't think there is a better meal than crispy chicken with a bright, tangy salad piled on top. This salad has a familiar flavor profile, but feels so much fresher than what you might find at a restaurant because it's filled with fresh herbs, tart, sweet, plump little mandarins, and a punchy vinaigrette. There is plenty of crisp and crunch in this salad—you're not going to miss the wonton strips, I promise.

PRODUCE

1 (3-inch/7.5 cm) piece peeled ginger

2 limes

½ head Napa or Savoy cabbage

1 bunch scallions

4 Kishu or 3 Satsuma mandarins

1 handful fresh mint leaves

DAIRY

2 large eggs, beaten

MEAT

2 boneless, skinless chicken breasts

PANTRY

1 cup (80 g) panko breadcrumbs

Kosher salt and freshly ground black pepper

2 tablespoons neutral oil, plus more for frying

¼ cup (60 ml) unseasoned rice vinegar

2 tablespoons toasted sesame oil

1 tablespoon sugar or honey

1 handful sliced almonds, toasted (see page 20)

COOK: Slice 2 chicken breasts in half lengthwise into 4 thin pieces. Place on a plastic cutting board, cover them in plastic wrap or parchment paper, and whack them with a rolling pin, wine bottle, or cast-iron skillet to thin them out until they are an even thickness of about ½ inch (12 mm).

Make a breading station with two pie plates or shallow bowls. Add 2 eggs to one plate, beating well with a fork or whisk, and 1 cup (80 g) breadcrumbs to the other. Season the breadcrumbs with salt and pepper. Using one hand, and one hand only, dip the chicken first in the egg, and let the excess drip off. Then dip in the breadcrumbs and set aside on a plate. Do this to all of the chicken. Get that cutting board in the sink and wash your hands and clean up anything raw chicken–related.

In a cast-iron or other large heavy skillet, heat ½ inch (12 mm) oil over medium-high heat. Check to see if it's ready by putting a breadcrumb in there—is it sizzling? Then it's ready. Fry your chicken for 2 to 3 minutes per side, until golden brown and cooked through.

Set aside on a wire cooling rack, sprinkling with a bit more salt.

MAKE THE CITRUSY GINGER VINAIGRETTE: Into a large bowl, grate a 3-inch (7.5 cm) piece peeled ginger with a Microplane to make 2 tablespoons. Add ¼ cup rice vinegar (60 ml), 2 tablespoons sesame oil, 1 tablespoon sugar or honey, juice of 1 lime, and 2 tablespoons neutral oil. Season with salt.

PREP: Core and shred ½ head cabbage using a mandoline. Slice 1 bunch scallions and peel and segment 3 or 4 mandarins. Cut the remaining lime into wedges for serving.

ASSEMBLE AND SERVE: Add the cabbage, scallions, mandarins, 1 handful mint leaves, and 1 handful toasted sliced almonds to the bowl with the dressing. Toss well. Put 2 pieces of chicken on each of the 2 serving plates. Top with the salad and serve with the lime wedges alongside.

immunity salad

SERVES 2 AS A LIGHT MEAL

(THIS IS GREAT SERVED WITH YOUR FAVORITE BROTHY SOUP.)

You don't need to already be sick to make this salad—but doesn't just looking at it brighten your day a little bit? Eating it regularly during the colder months gives your immune system a boost but also just feels really clean and fresh when we may be eating a lot of things that aren't.

PRODUCE

2 large beets

2 sweet potatoes

1 (1-inch/2.5 cm) piece ginger, peeled

1 clove garlic, peeled

1 head fennel

1 grapefruit

4 cups (80 g) baby spinach

PANTRY

Extra-virgin olive oil

Kosher salt and freshly ground black pepper

1 tablespoon apple cider vinegar

½ teaspoon honey

6 Medjool dates

½ cup (65 g) hulled pumpkin seeds (pepitas), toasted (see page 20)

COOK: Preheat the oven to 425°F (220°C).

Trim the leaves from 2 large beets (reserve for another use; for instance, sauté them in a little garlic and olive oil!). Roast according to the instructions on page 263.

When the beets have been in the oven for 20 minutes, slice 2 sweet potatoes in ¼-inch-thick (6 mm) rounds, place them on another rimmed baking sheet, and toss them with olive oil salt and pepper. Roast for about 30 minutes, tossing the potatoes once, until they are golden brown and the beets can be easily pierced with a knife. Let them cool to room temperature or until they are able to be handled.

MAKE THE GINGER, GARLIC, AND APPLE CIDER VINAIGRETTE: Into a large bowl, grate 1 inch (2.5 cm) ginger and 1 clove garlic, then add 1 tablespoon apple cider vinegar, ½ teaspoon honey, and 2 tablespoons olive oil. Season with salt and pepper.

PREP: Make an ice bath. Cut the stalks and fronds from the fennel bulb and cut in half, and then in half again, and then thinly slice on a mandoline right into the ice bath. Let crisp up for about 10 minutes, then pat dry on paper towels or a clean dish towel.

Cut 1 grapefruit into supremes (see page 37). Pit and slice 6 dates.

ASSEMBLE AND SERVE: Add the fennel, grapefruit, dates, 4 cups (80 g) baby spinach, beets, and sweet potatoes to the large bowl with the dressing. Toss everything to combine, arrange on serving plates, and then sprinkle with ½ cup (65 g) pumpkin seeds. And stay healthy!

swiss chard with garlicky yogurt and crispy egg

SERVES 2 AS A BREAKFAST

It's hard to play favorites, but I think chard is my favorite dark, leafy green—it's the one I always reach for in the market. Sure, it could be the vibrant stems that I'm a sucker for, but I also just like the way it tastes. It's not as earthy as kale, it's velvety when mixed with oil and runny egg yolk, and who knew greens for breakfast could feel so decadent?

Give the chard a good wash—maybe even more than once. Those dark leafy greens can be dirty!

PRODUCE
1 lemon

1 clove garlic, peeled

2 bunches
Swiss chard

DAIRY
¾ cup (180 ml) labneh
or Greek-style yogurt

2 to 4 large eggs
(depending on how
hungry you are!)

PANTRY
Kosher salt and
freshly ground
black pepper

Extra-virgin olive oil

Chili Crisp (page 260)

Toast, for serving

PREP: Put ¾ cup (180 ml) labneh in a small bowl. Use a Microplane to zest 1 lemon and 1 clove garlic into the yogurt. Stir to combine. Season with salt and pepper.

Strip the leaves of 2 bunches Swiss chard from their stems and tear the leaves into bite-size pieces. Chop the stems into ½-inch (12 mm) pieces.

COOK: In a cast-iron skillet, heat 1 tablespoon or so of oil over medium-high heat. Once the oil begins to shimmer, add your chard stems. Cook until they're beginning to get tender, about 3 minutes. Add the chard leaves and cook until wilted but not too wilty, still nice and green but softened, about 2 minutes. Squeeze the juice from the lemon that you zested into the pan, stir the greens around a bit, and then remove them with tongs and set aside.

Add a bit more oil to the pan, and once it's shimmering, crack the eggs in, two at a time. Sprinkle with a bit of salt and pepper and cook until the edges are nice and crispy brown and the whites are completely opaque, 2 to 3 minutes.

ASSEMBLE AND SERVE: Spoon a bit of the yogurt into a shallow bowl and put the greens on top, and then the eggs on top of that. Drizzle with a bit of chili crisp and dip your toast in it to scoop it all up.

roasted cauliflower with almonds, anchovies, and herbs

Every time I have made this dish for my partner, Ben, his reaction has been like he is trying it for the first time. Cauliflower can creep up on you like that. You can find a head of cauliflower in the back of your fridge that you don't even remember buying and with a few ingredients (that you most likely always have on hand) you can cook a meal that makes someone audibly "Mmm!" This dish will remind you how delicious cauliflower is, and it's in these little moments of appreciation where we can really feel the most present. If I have them on hand, I love tossing a few chopped dates into this dish at the end.

PRODUCE

2 heads cauliflower (Romanesco if you can find it, but it's not necessary)

Leaves of 1 bunch fresh parsley (about 2 cups leaves)

PANTRY

About 4 tablespoons (60 ml) extra-virgin olive oil

Kosher salt and freshly ground black pepper

½ cup (70 g) whole raw almonds

6 anchovies

1 tablespoon red wine vinegar

2 to 4 Medjool or Barhi dates, pitted and chopped (optional)

COOK: Preheat the oven to 425°F (220°C).

Remove all of the leaves from the cauliflower using your hands or a small knife, then break the cauliflower into florets. I like to use my hands for this, but a paring knife works great as well. Put the florets on a rimmed baking sheet—use a second sheet if your cauliflower was large to make sure you don't crowd the pieces. Add about 2 tablespoons oil (adding a bit more if you used a second sheet), tossing to coat, and season really well with salt and pepper.

Roast the cauliflower until deep golden brown and tender, tossing once, about 25 minutes. On another sheet pan, spread out ½ cup (70 g) almonds, then roast alongside the cauliflower for about 8 more minutes. Set a timer for the almonds.

MAKE THE ANCHOVY VINAIGRETTE: Chop 6 anchovies very finely and add them to a medium bowl. Add 1 tablespoon red wine vinegar and 2 tablespoons oil. Season with salt and pepper. Add a few chopped dates if you like! Whisk to combine.

ASSEMBLE AND SERVE: Roughly chop the toasted almonds and add to the bowl, along with the leaves of 1 bunch parsley. Toss to combine. Arrange the cauliflower on plates or a platter and top with the almond mixture.

crunchy citrus and chicories with turmeric tahini dressing

(TRY IT WITH GRILLED OR ROASTED CHICKEN OR SEARED SALMON)   SERVES 2 TO 4 AS A MEAL

I almost cut this recipe from the book because there are already a lot with chicories and citrus, but my friend Molly said she had been making it every week since she tested the recipe. Sweet, in-season citrus and crisp, bitter chicories just taste so good together. Here I use radicchio, one of the most commonly available chicories, but you could try any kind you prefer. The creamy, rich tahini dressing and abundance of seeds makes this a fulfilling meal, even without the addition of another type of protein.

PRODUCE

1 tablespoon lemon juice

6 small citrus, such as blood oranges, Satsumas, mandarins, or tangerines

1 head radicchio

Seeds from ½ large pomegranate (about ⅓ cup/60 g)

PANTRY

2 tablespoons tahini

¼ teaspoon turmeric powder

Kosher salt and freshly ground black pepper

4 Medjool or Barhi dates, pitted and sliced

1 handful roasted shelled pistachios, chopped

2 tablespoons toasted sesame seeds

1 tablespoon poppy seeds

MAKE THE TURMERIC TAHINI DRESSING: In a large bowl, whisk together 2 tablespoons tahini, ¼ teaspoon turmeric, and 1 tablespoon lemon juice. Add water, starting with 1 tablespoon and adding 1 teaspoon more at a time, until it is still fairly thick, but a drizzle-able consistency. Season with salt and pepper.

PREP: Using a small sharp knife or a serrated knife, remove the outer skin and pith from your citrus and either supreme or slice into thin rounds—a variety of shapes is best here. Simply peel and separate mandarins, if using. (See tip on styling citrus on page 39.)

Separate the leaves of the radicchio and tear into bite-size pieces; wash and spin dry.

ASSEMBLE AND SERVE: Put the radicchio in a bowl or onto plates or a platter. Drizzle with the dressing, keeping some on the side for serving. Scatter 4 sliced dates, the prepared citrus, and ⅓ cup (60 g) pomegranate seeds, and then sprinkle with 1 handful pistachios, 2 tablespoons sesame seeds, and 1 tablespoon poppy seeds.

roasted chicken and carrots with lentils and chili crisp

Even though I long to be crunchy in the way of having a pantry full of bulk-bin dried beans, I rarely remember to soak them until I've already begun cooking everything else in a dish. Enter the lentil, a quicker-cooking legume that is ready in about a half hour. If you want to feed a few more people, roast a whole chicken. Swap the chicken for feta cheese to make it vegetarian. Just don't forget the chili crisp: It warms this dish up and gives it an incredible amount of flavor.

PRODUCE

2 bunches baby or thin carrots (about 12 ounces/340 g)

2 small oranges

1 small head radicchio

MEAT

2 skin-on, bone-in chicken breasts (1¾ pounds/800 g)

PANTRY

1 cup (200 g) beluga or Le Puy lentils, rinsed

Kosher salt and freshly ground black pepper

4 tablespoons (60 ml) oil from Chili Crisp (page 260), plus the oil and crisp bits for serving

PREP: Peel 2 bunches baby carrots and cut them in half lengthwise. Peel 2 oranges and thinly slice into rounds. Separate the leaves of 1 head radicchio and tear into bite-size pieces; wash and spin dry.

COOK: Bring a small pot of water to a boil. Add 1 cup (200 g) lentils, reduce to a simmer, partially cover, and cook until there is just a little bit of tooth left, about 35 minutes for beluga, and slightly less for Le Puy. Season with salt and pepper.

Preheat the oven to 425°F (220°C).

Season 2 chicken breasts with salt and pepper. Heat a large ovenproof skillet over medium-high heat. Add a couple of tablespoons of the oil from the chili crisp (just the oil, not the crispy bits because they will burn!). Place the chicken, skin side down, in the pan and cook without moving it until the skin is deep golden brown, about 4 minutes. Flip the chicken over so the skin side is up and transfer the skillet to the oven. Roast the chicken until golden and cooked all the way through, 15 to 20 minutes (depending on the size). Set aside (leave the oven on).

Put the carrots and 2 tablespoons oil from the chili crisp (again: just the oil, not the crispy bits) on a rimmed baking sheet. Season with salt and pepper and toss around until coated. Roast until deep brown but not charred, 15 to 20 minutes.

ASSEMBLE AND SERVE: Scatter the lentils and radicchio on a serving plate. Place the carrots on top. Remove the chicken from the bones, cut it into thin slices, and snuggle these on top. Arrange the orange slices around the plate and top with a generous amount of chili crisp.

simple yet elegant endive

I love endive because of the way the dressing pools in its curved leaves. I love the way they look, and I love eating them. These bitter boys are the perfect match for toasted walnuts and a nutty Pecorino cheese—I would call this salad the definition of simple yet elegant.

PRODUCE

4 heads endive

1 lemon (Meyer lemon is very nice, if you can find it)

DAIRY

2 tablespoons butter

Pecorino cheese (preferably aged in walnut leaves, if you can find it)

PANTRY

2 handfuls raw walnuts

2 tablespoons plus ¼ cup (60 ml) toasted walnut oil

Kosher salt and freshly ground black pepper

2 tablespoons grainy mustard

½ teaspoon honey

PREP: Preheat the oven to 425°F (220°C). Put 2 handfuls walnuts on a rimmed baking sheet, along with 2 tablespoons oil, 2 tablespoons butter, and 2 tablespoons grated Pecorino and season with salt and pepper. Put them in the oven and set your timer for 6 minutes. Check them to see if they are golden brown and fragrant and add more time if necessary. Really set a timer—for some reason everyone always forgets about their toasted nuts.

Trim the bottoms of 4 heads endive and separate the leaves; wash and spin dry.

MAKE THE MEYER LEMON AND WALNUT VINAIGRETTE: In a medium bowl, whisk together ¼ cup (60 ml) oil, 2 tablespoons mustard, the juice and zest of 1 lemon, and ½ teaspoon honey. Season with salt and pepper.

ASSEMBLE AND SERVE: Pile a handful of the endive on a serving plate, making a base that you will continue to build on. Spoon a little of your vinaigrette onto the leaves, sprinkle with a bit of the toasted nuts, crushing them by hand as you go, and grate a little cloud of cheese with a Microplane as you continue to pile and dress the leaves to build a stack. The goal is for every leaf to have a little bit of everything on it. I like to finish my little mountain of endive with plenty of grated cheese and a bit of black pepper.

caesar salad pizza

My friend Shira said that her daughter Nova thought spreading the mustard on the raw dough of this pizza was a mistake, like the time I wore a jumpsuit with big pockets on the front and Nova thought I was wearing my pants backwards. But she ate it and thought it was magnificent, just like oversize patch pockets. I love that, and I love piling my pizza high with salad and making it feel healthier but still indulgent at the same time.

PRODUCE

1 clove garlic, peeled

2 lemons

½ head escarole (about 4 ounces/115 g)

DAIRY

Parmesan cheese

MEAT

6 boquerones or other good-quality anchovies packed in oil

PANTRY

1 pound (455 g) store-bought or homemade pizza dough

Flour for dusting

1 tablespoon Dijon mustard

Extra-virgin olive oil

Kosher salt and freshly ground black pepper

Flaky salt

PREP: Let pizza dough sit, covered, at room temperature for 30 minutes or up to an hour. It will be much easier to work with.

COOK: Preheat the oven to 500°F (260°C) with the racks in the upper and lower thirds and an upside-down rimmed baking sheet or a pizza stone on the bottom rack.

Make a 12-inch (30.5 cm) rectangle or a circle with the pizza dough on a lightly floured pizza peel or on parchment paper. Stretch it, spin it, roll it out with a wine bottle. Do what you have to do. Keep it rustic. Brush the dough with 1 tablespoon mustard. Grate 1 clove garlic with a Microplane over the dough and spread

it around. Drizzle with a couple of tablespoons of olive oil and sprinkle with kosher salt. Grate ¼ cup (25 g) cheese over the top of it. Slice 1 lemon as thinly as you can, remove the seeds, and arrange the lemon slices on the pizza. Open the oven and pull out the rack with the preheating baking sheet or stone. Transfer the pizza to the baking sheet or stone using a pizza peel, or onto parchment paper on another upside-down rimmed baking sheet or cookie sheet, so the pizza easily slides onto the preheating stone or baking sheet.

Bake until the crust is nice and golden, about 15 minutes. Remove it from the oven, slide the parchment (if using) out from under the pizza, and turn on your broiler.

Roughly chop ½ head (about 4 ounces/115 g) escarole, wash and spin dry, then pile it high on the pizza. Drizzle with a couple tablespoons of olive oil, and season with kosher salt and pepper. Return the pizza to the top rack this time, and if it's possible, keep the oven door open while you cook it because I don't know how strong your broiler is. Definitely don't walk away. This could take 2 minutes or 10, but you want a nice char on there.

ASSEMBLE AND SERVE: Arrange 6 boquerones all over the pizza. Grate lots of cheese, sprinkle flaky salt, and cut 1 lemon into wedges for serving.

STYLING TIP

This is pretty light as far as pizza goes but serving with plenty of lemon wedges really brightens it up and makes it—and anything at all—look even more fresh and appealing. Cut lemons or limes in half lengthwise (from tip to tip) and then lengthwise again into sleeker wedges or width-wise into smaller smiley looking "Weeble-Wobbles" for a different look.

chicories and persimmons

SERVES 2 TO 4 AS A STARTER OR SIDE

This is inspired by another salad at the Four Horsemen, my favorite restaurant. I know that's two in a row, but I've probably spent one year's salary on food and wine there, so I don't think it will be a problem. I love you guys!

PRODUCE

2 heads mixed chicories, such as red endive, whatever the pink one is actually called, and Castlefranco

2 Fuyu persimmons

1 lemon

DAIRY

¼ cup (60 ml) buttermilk

PANTRY

1 handful walnuts

1 tablespoon plus 1 teaspoon maple syrup

3 tablespoons extra-virgin olive oil

Pinch cayenne pepper

Kosher salt and freshly ground black pepper

2 tablespoons white balsamic vinegar

COOK: Preheat the oven to 350°F (175°C).

In a small bowl, combine 1 handful walnuts, 1 tablespoon maple syrup, 1 tablespoon oil, and a sprinkle of cayenne and salt and toss to coat. Transfer to a parchment-lined rimmed baking sheet. Cook for 8 to 10 minutes, until toasted and bubbling. Set a timer!

PREP: Separate the leaves of 2 heads chicory and tear into bite-size pieces; wash and spin dry. Cut persimmons in half, remove seeds, and thinly slice.

MAKE THE WHITE BALSAMIC AND BUTTERMILK DRESSING: In a small bowl, mix together ¼ cup (60 ml) buttermilk, 2 tablespoons oil, 2 tablespoons white balsamic vinegar, the zest and juice of 1 lemon, and 1 teaspoon maple syrup and season with salt and pepper.

ASSEMBLE AND SERVE: Drizzle the chicories with the dressing and arrange on a serving plate. Crush the candied walnuts with your hands over the top of the salad and place the persimmons throughout the leaves.

shaved fennel and tuna salad

SERVES 2 AS A MEAL

A quick lunch or a way to clean out the fridge, this salad, built with ingredients that you probably have on hand and that last for a long time, feels light, fresh, and delicious. It's also really nice with supremed orange or grapefruit segments in place of apples, if that's what you happen to have, and any other crunchy things buried in the fridge that can be thinly sliced, like cucumbers or radishes. Want to make it fancy? Add a little pinch of saffron to the lemon juice and let it sit for a few seconds before making the vinaigrette. Use a mandoline to make quick work of all the slicing (and make it look even more elegant by making everything whisper thin).

PREP: Trim and quarter 1 head fennel. Slice the fennel and 2 stalks celery on a mandoline so they are about the thickness of a quarter. Add the shavings to a salad spinner filled with ice water, along with the leaves from the whole head of celery and allow to crisp up while you prep the rest of the salad. Trim the bottom of 1 head endive, thinly slice the leaves, and add to the salad spinner. Thinly slice 1 apple on the mandoline and set aside.

MAKE THE DATE-SWEETENED VINAIGRETTE: Finely chop 2 dates and sort of mash them up with a fork or a whisk in the bottom of a large bowl. Squeeze the juice of ½ lemon into the bowl and whisk in ¼ cup (60 ml) oil. Season with salt and pepper.

ASSEMBLE AND SERVE: Spin the fennel, celery, and endive until dry then add to the bowl with the dressing. Add the sliced apple, and 1 big handful parsley leaves and toss to combine. Plate the salad and top with the tuna. Serve topped with a few cracks of black pepper and the remaining ½ lemon cut into wedges.

PRODUCE	PANTRY
1 head fennel	2 very soft dates, such as fancy Medjool
2 stalks celery, plus leaves from the whole head	¼ cup (60 ml) extra-virgin olive oil
1 head endive	Kosher salt and freshly ground black pepper
1 apple (I like Honey Crisp), cored	1 (6.7-ounce/190 g) jar pole-caught tuna packed in oil, drained
1 lemon	
1 big handful fresh parsley leaves	

raw and roasted caesar brussels sprouts

One time my friend Glennis asked me if Pecorino is a meat, and no, it's not, but I think this cheese is savory and satisfying enough when paired with walnuts that these Brussels sprouts don't need any bacon, or anything else. This recipe asks you to prepare the Brussels in not one, but two ways, which might seem annoying, but I promise you, it's worth it. This salad will make you truly appreciate the unique qualities of the Brussels sprout, a deeply underrated vegetable.

PRODUCE

1 pound (455 g) Brussels sprouts

2 lemons (Meyer lemon, if you can find it)

DAIRY

Pecorino cheese

PANTRY

1 cup (100 g) walnuts

Extra-virgin olive oil

Kosher salt and freshly ground black pepper

1 tablespoon grainy mustard

1 tablespoon mayonnaise

3 anchovies, finely chopped

PREP: Preheat the oven to 450°F (230°C).

Trim the bottom and separate the leaves from the base of ½ pound (225 g) Brussels sprouts. The outer leaves will peel off nicely, and then you kind of have to start ripping them apart, and that's okay. Add the leaves to a rimmed baking sheet and set aside. Trim the bottoms off the remaining ½ pound (225 g) Brussels sprouts and slice them whisper-thin. If you are an advanced and confident user, you could employ a mandoline for this. If you have a shredding attachment on your food processor, you could use that too, but doing it by hand really isn't so bad either.

COOK: Add 1 cup (100 g) walnuts to the rimmed baking sheet with Brussels leaves and drizzle with olive oil and season with salt and pepper. Roast, tossing once, until charred in places and the walnuts are toasty and fragrant, about 10 minutes. Set a timer!

MAKE THE ALMOST CAESAR DRESSING: In a large bowl, whisk together the zest and juice of 1 lemon, 1 tablespoon mustard, 1 tablespoon mayonnaise, and 3 finely chopped anchovies until fully combined. Season with salt and pepper.

ASSEMBLE AND SERVE: Toss everything together in the bowl with the dressing. Finely grate ½ cup (50 g) Pecorino right into the bowl, toss, transfer to a serving dish or platter, and top with more cheese. Cut the remaining lemon into wedges to serve on the side.

bright and crunchy salmon

Tender salmon pairs perfectly with super-crunchy textures and bold, bright, and tangy flavors in this fresh dish. This salad borrows flavors from some of my favorite Thai dishes, but it is a healthy meal you can make at home in minutes.

PRODUCE

1 orange, such as Cara Cara or blood

1 lime

1 tablespoon Lacto-Fermented Fresno Chiles (page 256), or 1 thinly sliced fresh jalapeño or serrano chile

1 recipe Frizzled Shallots (page 261), plus 1½ cups (360 ml) reserved shallot oil

1 watermelon radish (or 3 smaller radishes)

3 Persian cucumbers

1 big handful fresh mint leaves, cilantro leaves, and Thai basil leaves

MEAT

12 ounces (340 g) wild salmon fillet, cut into 2 portions

PANTRY

Kosher salt

Extra-virgin olive oil

1 tablespoon rice vinegar

1 tablespoon fish sauce

½ cup (75 g) roasted and salted skin-on peanuts

½ cup (15 g) crispy rice cereal

COOK: Preheat the oven to 325°F (165°C).

Cut ½ orange and ½ lime into thin slices and put in a 9-inch (23 cm) square baking dish, a small, rimmed baking sheet, or even a heatproof skillet.

Place 12 ounces (340 g) salmon on top and sprinkle with salt and 1 tablespoon pickled chiles. Pour all but 2 tablespoons of the reserved shallot oil over the salmon. Bake until the salmon is opaque throughout, about 25 minutes. Remove from the oil, and once cool enough to touch, break into bite-size pieces.

PREP: Use the mandoline to thinly slice 1 watermelon radish and set in a bowl of ice water until the slices are extra crunchy. Slice 3 Persian cucumbers and put in a large bowl.

MAKE THE LIME AND FISH SAUCE VINAIGRETTE: Into a small bowl or measuring cup, juice the remaining ½ orange and ½ lime; add 1 tablespoon rice vinegar, 1 tablespoon fish sauce, and the 2 tablespoons reserved shallot oil; taste for seasoning.

ASSEMBLE AND SERVE: Dry off the radishes and add to the bowl of cucumbers. Add the flaked salmon and 1 big handful herbs, drizzle with just a few tablespoons of the dressing, and toss, being careful not to overdress. Serve the rest of the dressing on the side to preserve the crunchiness of the ingredients. Put on serving plates or a platter and top with frizzled shallots, ½ cup (75 g) peanuts, and ½ cup (15 g) crispy rice creal.

Tea-Smoked Chicken and
Bitter Greens (page 72)

tea-smoked chicken and bitter greens

SERVES 4 AS A MEAL, WITH LEFTOVER CHICKEN AND BROTH

Now, you may look at this recipe and be intimidated, but let me begin by saying I once saw Martha tea smoke a whole chicken in the middle of the night, or at least what seemed like it. It involves a few steps, but they are simple techniques that yield a really, really special finished result. The chicken will be extremely moist on the inside, and a beautiful shiny deep golden on the outside. It will fill the house with the most wonderful aromas, and while it's a technique that has a long history in China, I feel like it will be a refreshing new take on chicken to most. This technique can be done in a wok, a Dutch oven, or a stock pot—anything that a steamer rack can fit in, a chicken can fit in, and has a lid to cover it. For this recipe you'll just use the chicken breast, which you will thinly slice on a diagonal to make as elegant as possible. You could shred the dark meat and add to the salad if you want additional protein, or save it for a snack (it makes a great lettuce cup filler). Better yet, save the poaching liquid and make a beautiful brothy soup.

PRODUCE

1 yellow onion, cut in half

1 head garlic, cut in half

1 (2-inch/5 cm) piece ginger, peeled and sliced

1 head endive

1 small Asian pear

3 cups (85 g) baby mustard greens

MEAT

1 whole chicken (3½ to 4 pounds/ 1.6 to 1.8 kg)

PANTRY

2 teaspoons Sichuan peppercorns

5 star anise

Kosher salt

Soy sauce

4 whole chiles japones, crushed (or ½ teaspoon crushed red pepper flakes)

¼ cup (55 g) dark brown sugar

½ cup (90 g) uncooked long-grain white rice

¼ cup (20 g) loose-leaf black tea, such as oolong

2 tablespoons toasted almond (or sesame) oil, plus some for brushing

1 teaspoon Dijon mustard

1 tablespoon white balsamic vinegar

½ teaspoon honey

Freshly ground black pepper

½ cup (50 g) sliced almonds, toasted (see page 20)

PREP: At least 4 hours or up to one night in advance, make the brine for the chicken: In a mortar and pestle or spice grinder, grind 1 teaspoon Sichuan peppercorns, 1 star anise, and 2 tablespoons salt into a powder with an even consistency. Rub it all over 1 whole chicken, wrap in plastic, and return to the fridge.

COOK: Remove the chicken from the fridge and let sit at room temperature for about 15 minutes. Place the chicken, breast side down, in a stockpot and cover with water. Add 1 halved onion, 1 halved head of garlic, sliced 2-inch (5 cm) piece ginger, and 2 star anise. Bring to a boil. Lower to a simmer and cook until the chicken reads 165°F (74°C) on an instant-read thermometer, about 1 hour. Carefully remove from the liquid, put on a rimmed baking sheet to cool slightly, and brush with a couple of tablespoons of soy sauce.

Line your smoking vessel of choice (wok, Dutch oven, stock pot, etc.) with heavy aluminum foil. Combine 4 crushed chile japones, 2 crushed star anise, 1 teaspoon Sichuan peppercorns, ¼ cup (55 g) brown sugar, ½ cup (90 g) white rice, and ¼ cup (20 g) black tea leaves in a small bowl, then add to the bottom of the pot, smoothing it out into an even layer. Place your steaming rack over the mixture and place your chicken, breast side up, on the rack. Cover the pot and turn the heat up to medium-high. Cook for 15 minutes, then remove from the heat and let the chicken sit for 15 more minutes with the lid sealed.

When you open the smoker, the chicken should be a brilliant golden brown. Brush it with a bit of toasted almond oil and let cool while you make the rest of the salad.

MAKE THE WHITE BALSAMIC, ALMOND OIL, AND HONEY VINAIGRETTE: In a small bowl, whisk to combine 1 teaspoon mustard, 1 tablespoon white balsamic vinegar, ½ teaspoon honey, and 2 tablespoons toasted almond oil and season with salt and pepper.

When the chicken has cooled enough to touch, you'll need to remove the breasts. With the neck of the chicken facing away from you with the breast side up, pop the legs off the chicken first, by bending them away from the body and down toward the board until the joint pops (you'll hear it/feel it), then use a knife to cleanly cut through the skin. Now, for the breasts, feel for the hard ridge down the center of the breasts, then start to carve slightly to the side of the center from the top of the bird to the bottom to gently free the breast meat from the bone. Spin the bird around to repeat this process on the other side. Once you have the two breasts free, thinly slice them on a diagonal. Reserve the dark meat for another use.

ASSEMBLE AND SERVE: Separate the leaves of 1 head endive and tear into bite-size pieces; wash and spin dry. Thinly slice 1 Asian pear. Arrange 3 cups (85 g) baby mustard greens, the endive, and pear on a platter, then arrange the sliced chicken breast on top. Drizzle with the dressing and sprinkle with ½ cup (50 g) toasted sliced almonds.

little gem with creamy dressing, hazelnuts, and petals

SERVES 4 AS A STARTER OR SIDE

Little Gem has an unbeatable crunch and feels fresh and light, even when smothered in a creamy dressing. Ever since I made this dressing for my friend David and told him the secret ingredient was mayonnaise, he thinks everything I make has mayonnaise in it, but it's just not true . . . not really, at least. This makes a great side dish to any holiday meal that needs some leafy greens on the table.

PRODUCE

1 lemon

4 small heads Little Gem lettuce

1 handful fresh mint leaves

Petals from edible flowers such as nasturtium, calendula, or marigold

DAIRY

½ tablespoon unsalted butter

2 tablespoons grated Pecorino cheese, plus more for grating on top later

PANTRY

1 big handful hazelnuts

1 tablespoon extra-virgin olive oil

Kosher salt and freshly ground black pepper

3 tablespoons mayonnaise

COOK: Preheat the oven to 350°F (175°C).

On a rimmed baking sheet, toss 1 big handful hazelnuts, ½ tablespoon butter, 1 tablespoon oil, 2 tablespoons Pecorino, and a bit of salt and pepper. Bake for about 8 minutes, until nice and golden. Set a timer! Cool a little bit and roughly chop.

MAKE THE CREAMY LEMON DRESSING: Whisk together 3 tablespoons mayonnaise, the zest and juice of 1 lemon, and a bit of salt and pepper until completely smooth and combined.

PREP: Separate the leaves of 4 heads lettuce and tear into bite-size pieces; wash and spin dry.

ASSEMBLE AND SERVE: Toss the lettuce and dressing in a large bowl. Transfer to serving plates or a platter and scatter with 1 handful mint leaves, the toasted hazelnuts, and more cheese, if desired.

STYLING TIP

Edible flowers can elevate a really simple salad into something special, especially for holidays and occasions. Many of them add wonderful flavor too—my favorites are nasturtiums and coriander blossoms, which are both quite common, especially if you have a garden at home. Chive and garlic blossoms are other favorites that provide flavor, but check your famers' market and even your grocery store; most places have at least a little something.

steak salad to change your mood

Nine times out of ten, if I am in a bad mood, it's because I am hungry. Whether you're starting to come undone, or you just want to make a satisfying meal to share with someone special, this is a classic combination that is sure to do the trick.

PRODUCE

½ pound (225 g) baby Yukon gold potatoes

1 cup (40 g) Frizzled Shallots (page 261), plus 4 tablespoons (60 ml) reserved shallot oil

3 cups (60 g) baby arugula

2 tablespoons thinly sliced chives

MEAT

2 filets mignons, about 2 inches (5 cm) thick (about ¾ pound/340 g)

PANTRY

Kosher salt and freshly ground black pepper

1 tablespoon grainy mustard

1 tablespoon mayonnaise

1 teaspoon prepared horseradish

1 teaspoon sherry vinegar

PREP: Preheat the oven to 425°F (220°C).

Generously season 2 filets mignons with salt and pepper and allow to come to room temperature (about 30 minutes).

MAKE THE HORSERADISH DRESSING: In a small bowl, combine 1 tablespoon mustard, 1 tablespoon mayonnaise, 1 teaspoon horseradish, 1 teaspoon sherry vinegar, and about 2 tablespoons of the reserved shallot oil. Season with salt and pepper.

Cut ½ pound (225 g) baby potatoes into halves.

COOK: Put the potatoes on a rimmed baking sheet, tossing with 1 tablespoon of the reserved shallot oil and plenty of salt and pepper. Roast until deep golden brown, 25 minutes.

Heat a skillet (preferably cast-iron) over medium-high to high heat—closer to high. Drizzle 1 tablespoon of the reserved shallot oil and swirl it around in the pan. Once it's shimmering like the ocean receding from the shore after a wave has crashed, it's time to add your steaks to the pan. Keep it this hot unless the pan really starts to smoke like crazy, then you can turn it down a bit, but definitely turn your exhaust hood on. Cook the steaks for about 4 minutes on each side for medium-rare. The best way to test this if you're feeling nervous is to use an instant-read thermometer (it takes all the guesswork out of cooking meat); medium-rare should read 135°F (57°C), and medium will be 145°F (63°C). Transfer the steak to a cutting board and let rest for a few minutes, then slice thinly against the grain.

ASSEMBLE AND SERVE: Arrange 3 cups (60 g) arugula on plates or a platter, and snuggle in the potatoes everywhere. Drizzle with the dressing. Lift the thinly sliced steak using your knife, and shingle it/fan it out over the arugula. Sprinkle with the crispy shallots and chives.

todas las frutas

SERVES 2 TO 4

AS A BREAKFAST OR DESSERT

This fruit salad can be anything, taking advantage of the produce wherever you happen to be. This particular combination of flavors reminds me of Mexico City, a place I like to visit often, and can be specially nice during the dead of winter. It's bold, colorful, intensely sweet, familiar but a little bit different, just like the city itself.

PRODUCE

3 tiny bananas

2 red or black plums

4 kumquats

1 very ripe peeled mango

4 ripe loquats or guava

2 passion fruits

1 handful blackberries

Juice of 2 Mexican or key limes

PREP: Thinly slice 3 tiny bananas, 2 plums, 4 kumquats, and 1 peeled mango. Cut 4 loquats in half, removing the pits. Halve 2 passion fruits and scoop out the pulp and seeds; discard the rind.

ASSEMBLE AND SERVE: Arrange the bananas, plums, kumquats, mango, loquats, and 1 handful blackberries on a platter. Top with the passion fruit pulp and seeds and squeeze the juice of 2 limes over the whole thing.

jicama slaw

SERVES 4 AS A SIDE

Jicama is delicious. A little sweet and extremely crispy and juicy, it's delicious on top of a fish taco—or any taco, really. It's delicious alongside a piece of fish or a grilled skirt steak, or with ceviche. It's delicious sliced and eaten plain—but it's even more delicious when combined with lime, radishes, avocado, and cilantro like it is in this recipe.

PRODUCE

1 medium jicama (about 1¼ pounds/570 g)

1 bunch radishes

1 lime

1 avocado

½ cup (15 g) fresh cilantro leaves

PANTRY

Extra-virgin olive oil

Kosher salt and freshly ground black pepper

A sprinkle of ancho chile powder

PREP: Peel 1 jicama. I think it's easiest to peel a jicama by cutting off the ends so that it lays flat and then cutting along the sides with a knife, losing as little of the flesh as possible. This is one thing I recommend julienning by hand; every other method just doesn't quite work. But use your mandoline to very thinly slice 1 bunch radishes right into the bowl. Juice 1 lime right into the bowl and drizzle a tablespoon or two of oil, just enough to lightly coat everything, right in there. Season with salt and pepper.

ASSEMBLE AND SERVE: Transfer the jicama mixture to a serving plate. Halve, pit, peel, and thinly slice 1 avocado and arrange around the plate. Sprinkle with ½ cup (15 g) cilantro leaves and ancho chile powder. Serve right away, as it can get kind of soggy.

When I think of spring, I think of green. When I think of green I think of the smell of grass and the feeling of it underfoot, and the yellow-tinged leaves bursting from the buds of the trees lining my street. I think of how the light against my white bedroom walls changes, and the feeling of the warmth of the sun on my shoulders.

When I think of spring, I think of winter ending. I think of new beginnings. I think of emerging from a darkness, taking a leap, letting go. I think of the rain that comes in droplets and clings to my windows and eventually releases to the concrete. I think about falling too—releasing. I think of all those cold, gray days and the ways the golds and greens begin to pop against the sidewalks and buildings. The spring is precious and brief; spring is fleeting.

I think of young lettuces, asparagus, and spinach, and I think of peas. Freshness, the taste of green itself. New, tender, sweet.

carrots for lauryn

SERVES 2 TO 4 AS A STARTER OR SIDE

Carrots, really good carrots, have the sweetest flavor and the unique freshness of just coming out of the earth. Usually this sweetness is just used in recipes to offset stronger flavors in soups and sauces—but a farm-fresh carrot needs very little to shine on its own. When my friend Lauryn was pregnant, all she wanted was butter and this salad. I never made it for her, and I deeply regret it. But I've made it for her now, and I gave her my julienne peeler so she can make it for herself whenever she wants. The julienne peeler is a gift to us all, really.

MAKE THE LEMON AND MUSTARD VINAIGRETTE: In a large bowl, whisk together 2 tablespoons mustard, ¼ cup (60 ml) oil, and the zest and juice of 1 lemon. Season with salt and pepper.

PREP, ASSEMBLE, AND SERVE: Peel and julienne 4 carrots and add to the bowl with the dressing. Roughly chop 1 handful parsley and add to the bowl. Season to taste and toss to combine. You're done; that's it. Really.

PRODUCE

1 lemon

4 medium to large carrots

1 handful fresh parsley

PANTRY

2 tablespoons grainy mustard

¼ cup (60 ml) extra-virgin olive oil

Kosher salt and freshly ground black pepper

carrot and saffron socca

My ex-boyfriend Phillip has a Piper Cherokee from the 1960s named "Lady Whiskey" that is practically held together by two screws. We flew everywhere in it, but one summer, he flew us to Maine and then we took a little boat to Cushing Island to spend a few summer days with his friend Beroush, the Saffron King, and his family. What a thing to be the king of, the most expensive spice in the world. Saffron—a beautiful color and with a floral and earthy flavor—is something I love so much that I drink it like tea with a little honey. Don't skimp here. Splurge on the real deal and use just a pinch. Blooming the saffron in warm water allows its striking color and flavor to deepen, making sure you get the most out of this treasure.

This socca, or chickpea pancake, is a beautiful way to experience saffron's unique flavor. I love how it pairs with sweet carrots and slightly bitter carrot tops. It's an elegant departure from pizza. Hold the cheese for a completely gluten-free and vegan meal.

PRODUCE
1 bunch carrots with tops

2 lemons

3 radishes

3 scallions

1 handful fresh dill

DAIRY
⅓ cup (50 g) crumbled feta cheese

Yogurt, for serving

PANTRY

FOR THE SOCCA:

Big pinch saffron

1 cup (240 ml) lukewarm water

1 cup (90 g) chickpea flour

1 teaspoon kosher salt

¼ cup (60 ml) plus 2 tablespoons extra-virgin olive oil

FOR THE PESTO AND THE SALAD:

Kosher salt

⅓ cup (75 ml) extra-virgin olive oil

¼ teaspoon ground cinnamon

½ cup (50 g) sliced almonds, toasted (see page 20)

Crushed red pepper flakes

Preheat the oven to 450°F (220°C) with a 12-inch (30.5 cm) cast-iron skillet or round griddle inside.

PREPARE THE SOCCA BATTER: Add a big pinch of saffron to 1 cup (240 ml) lukewarm water and let steep for a few moments. In a medium bowl, whisk together 1 cup (90 g) chickpea flour and 1 teaspoon salt, then add the saffron water and ¼ cup (60 ml) oil. Whisk until smooth and set aside while you prepare your pesto.

MAKE THE PESTO: Bring a medium pot of salted water to a boil and prepare an ice bath. Remove the tops from 1 bunch carrots, pinching off any tough or stiff stems. Rinse the tops well in a bowl of water—these tend to be quite dirty; you might have to do this a couple of times. Once clean, add to the boiling water and cook for about 30 seconds, until they are bright green. Transfer to the ice bath.

Once cool, remove the tops from the ice bath, squeeze out excess moisture, and then spread onto a clean towel or paper towels to dry completely. Finely chop and put in a small bowl. Stir in ⅓ cup (75 ml) oil, the zest and juice of 1 lemon, and ¼ teaspoon cinnamon, and season with salt.

PREP: Using a Y-peeler or a mandoline, create thin ribbons from the carrots. Thinly slice the radishes. Add both veggies to the ice bath to crisp up while you cook the socca. Slice the scallions.

MAKE THE SOCCA: Carefully remove the preheated pan from the oven and place on top of the stove. Add 2 tablespoons olive oil and the scallions and cook until softened, 3 to 4 minutes. Carefully pour in the batter and return the pan to the oven. Bake until golden brown and completely set, 10 to 12 minutes. Broil for about 2 minutes for additional color.

ASSEMBLE AND SERVE: Drain and pat the carrots and radishes dry and add to a medium bowl. Toss with a few spoonfuls of the pesto, ½ cup (50 g) almonds, ⅓ cup (50 g) cheese, and the dill. Scatter this mixture on top of the socca and serve with some red pepper flakes, lemon wedges, and yogurt on the side.

shaved radish breakfast salad with jammy eggs and dukkah

I'm a slow riser, you might even say lazy in the mornings, and for me, making a breakfast salad is a wonderful way to ease into the day. Salad for breakfast? You might wonder, but this isn't about eating a bowl full of lettuce the minute you open your eyes. Fresh, crunchy, peppery radishes with salty and rich feta cheese and eggs with runny yolks are the perfect thing to accompany dukkah here, a traditional Egyptian spice and nut mix. Did you know Egyptians began cultivating radishes even before the pyramids were built?

COOK: Bring water to a boil in a small pot and prepare an ice bath. Carefully add the eggs to the water and boil for 7 minutes. Transfer to the ice bath.

PREP: Thinly slice 1 bunch radishes on a mandoline to about the thickness of a coin and add to the ice bath for a minute or two to crisp up. Pat dry on paper towels. Thinly slice 7 ounces (200 g) cheese.

ASSEMBLE AND SERVE: On a serving plate or platter, arrange the sliced feta and radishes, then sprinkle with the leaves from 1 small bunch mint. Peel the eggs, cut in half lengthwise, and nuzzle them among the mint leaves. Drizzle with a generous glug of oil, flaky salt, pepper, and about ¼ cup (30 g) dukkah. Serve with (or on) a few slices of toast.

PRODUCE
1 bunch radishes (about 12 ounces/340 g)

1 bunch fresh mint (about 2 handfuls leaves)

DAIRY
4 large eggs

7 ounces (200 g) good feta cheese (Valbreso or French)

PANTRY
Extra-virgin olive oil

Flaky salt and freshly ground black pepper

About ¼ cup (30 g) Dukkah (page 261)

Sourdough (or your other favorite toast), for serving

asparagus, peas, and cucumber "cacio e pepe"

I won't try to say this is anything like eating pasta cacio e pepe or that it will satisfy your craving for it—because it isn't, and it won't. But there is something ethereal about this salad that really speaks to the season. Shaved vegetables are so elegant and fresh. You could also add some raw zucchini noodles in place of cucumber if you wanted to, serve it on top of thin, crispy or grilled chicken cutlets, or you could pile it on top of baked pizza crust (I might add a little burrata if I was doing that).

PRODUCE

1 cup (145 g) shelled fresh (or frozen) English peas

2 Persian cucumbers, or 1 English cucumber

1 pound (455 g) asparagus

1 lemon

1 clove garlic

1 handful arugula

DAIRY

Parmesan cheese

Pecorino cheese

PANTRY

Extra-virgin olive oil

Kosher salt and freshly ground black pepper

COOK: Boil water in a small pot and salt it heavily. Prepare an ice bath with a fine-mesh sieve set over it to contain your peas. Add 1 cup (145 g) peas to the boiling water and boil until the peas are crisp-tender and bright green. Strain and transfer to the ice bath.

PREP: Trim the ends off 2 Persian cucumbers or 1 English cucumber and shave into long ribbons using a Y-peeler. Add them to the ice bath to crisp up.

Preheat the broiler with the rack about 4 inches (10 cm) from the heating element.

Using a Y-peeler, peel 1 pound (455 g) asparagus from root end to tip. When you get down to where you can't peel anymore, trim off the ends and discard, and transfer the peelings to a rimmed baking sheet.

COOK: Drizzle the asparagus with a bit of oil and season with salt and lots of black pepper. Toss well to coat. Broil until just charred—about 4 minutes.

MAKE THE LEMON GARLIC VINAIGRETTE: In a large bowl, combine the juice of ½ lemon and about ¼ cup (60 ml) oil, and grate the garlic clove into the mixture.

ASSEMBLE AND SERVE: Drain and pat dry the cucumbers and add them to the bowl with the dressing, along with 1 handful arugula, the asparagus, and peas. Transfer to serving plates or a platter. Grate a fluffy cloud of Parmesan and Pecorino cheeses over the top and stir everything together before taking your first bite.

STYLING TIP
With any shaved vegetable, give everything a little "fluffing up" using a scrunching and lifting motion as you add handfuls to the plate so the dish has volume and doesn't fall flat.

roasted salmon with pistachios and pea tendrils

One time I was driving from Bed-Stuy to Williamsburg (which is a very short but stressful drive) and I was listening to NPR and had to pull over when Diana Henry had a revelation that there is nothing that tastes like a pistachio, and a pistachio doesn't taste like anything else, and when combined with the freshness, the newness of a pea, it is something so special. Experience the combination for yourself in this meal that comes together fast enough to make on a weeknight but is fancy enough for a dinner party.

PRODUCE

½ pound (225 g) sugar snap peas

¼ pound (115 g) snow peas

1 small bunch (about ¼ pound/115 g) pea tendrils (baby spinach and arugula are good substitutes)

2 lemons

DAIRY

2 tablespoons crème fraîche

MEAT

4 (6-ounce/170 g) portions wild salmon fillet, skin removed

PANTRY

Kosher salt and freshly ground black pepper

2 tablespoons grainy mustard

⅓ cup (50 g) finely chopped pistachios

1 tablespoon white balsamic vinegar

2 tablespoons extra-virgin olive oil

PREP: Preheat the oven to 325°F (165°C).

Remove the strings of ½ pound (225 g) sugar snap peas. Halve some on the bias. Trim ¼ pound (115 g) snow peas and remove the thick stems of the pea tendrils.

Place 4 (6-ounce/170 g) salmon portions on paper towels and pat dry. Season well with salt and pepper. In a small cup, stir together 1 tablespoon crème fraîche and 2 tablespoons mustard. Place the salmon, what used to be the skin side down, in a 9 by 13-inch (23 by 33 cm) baking dish or a rimmed baking sheet and smear the crème fraîche mixture on top. Sprinkle ⅓ cup (50 g) chopped pistachios on top to coat the fish.

COOK: Bake the salmon for 20 to 25 minutes, until completely opaque up the sides of the fish. (If you like your salmon on the medium-rare side, you could go for about 15 minutes.)

Bring a small pot of water to a boil and prepare an ice bath. Blanch your sugar snap peas until crisp tender and bright green, about 2 minutes, and transfer to the ice bath using a spider or tongs. Now blanch your snow peas for about 1 minute and transfer to the ice bath.

MAKE THE CRÈME FRAÎCHE DRESSING: In a small bowl, combine the zest and juice of 1 lemon, 1 tablespoon white balsamic vinegar, 1 tablespoon crème fraîche, and 2 tablespoons olive oil and season well with salt and pepper.

ASSEMBLE AND SERVE: Drain and dry the peas on paper towels before combining with the pea tendrils and the dressing in a large serving bowl. Serve the pea mixture alongside the salmon with lemon wedges.

burrata with favas, peas, and preserved lemon

SERVES 4 TO 6 AS A STARTER OR SIDE (THIS IS EXCELLENT WITH LAMB.)

When English peas are in season and finally sweet, I can't get enough of eating them straight out of their shells. Squeezing the fava beans out of their little jackets is pretty fun too—I love the moment the skin splits to reveal the brightest, most amazing green inside. This simple dish is so beautiful and clean and allows the flavors of the favas and peas to shine.

PRODUCE

1 cup (170 g) shelled fava beans, preferably fresh from 1½ pounds (680 g) beans

2 cups (290 g) shelled English peas, preferably fresh from 1½ pounds (680 g) peas

Fresh chive blossoms (or just some chopped chives, mint, or other fresh herbs)

DAIRY

2 balls burrata (about 8 ounces/225 g)

PANTRY

Kosher salt and freshly ground black pepper

2 tablespoons finely chopped preserved lemon

Extra-virgin olive oil (use your very good kind)

Flaky salt

COOK: In a small pot, bring heavily salted water to a boil. Prepare an ice bath with a fine-mesh sieve placed over the bowl (to contain your beans and peas). Blanch 1 cup (170 g) favas for 3 to 5 minutes. Transfer to the ice bath, and then to a paper towel–lined plate.

Boil 2 cups (290 g) peas for 3 to 5 minutes, until crisp-tender and bright green. Transfer to the ice bath. Once cool, transfer to a paper towel–lined plate. Unzip all of your fava beans by squeezing them out of their jackets to reveal the beautiful, bright green pod within.

ASSEMBLE AND SERVE: Transfer all of the fava beans and peas to a serving bowl. Add the 2 balls burrata and sprinkle 2 tablespoons finely chopped preserved lemon over everything. Drizzle with your very good olive oil and grind plenty of black pepper over it. Sprinkle with flaky salt and chive blossoms or fresh herbs.

a tender salad

SERVES 2 TO 4 AS A LIGHT MEAL, OR PAIR WITH A DELICATE FISH, ROASTED LAMB, OR POACHED CHICKEN

This is a powerful salad. It's symbolic of the spring itself. It reminds me of the magical quality that you can feel, thick in the air before a warm rain shower. I remember sending a photo of this salad in those critical first few text message exchanges with someone, filled with complete ecstasy when he agreed to meet for dinner.

PRODUCE

2 heads Little Gem lettuce

1 bunch adolescent arugula

1 handful pea tendrils

½ pound (225 g) shelled English peas

½ pound (225 g) sugar snap peas

1 lemon

2 tablespoons finely chopped fresh chives, plus some blossoms

1 handful fresh mint leaves

DAIRY

1 egg yolk

PANTRY

½ teaspoon Dijon mustard

½ cup (120 ml) good extra-virgin olive oil

Nutritional yeast

Kosher salt and freshly ground black pepper

Quick-Pickled Chive Blossoms (page 256) or garlic chive blossoms

Handful roasted salted almonds, chopped

Crushed red pepper flakes

PREP: Separate the leaves of 2 heads lettuce and tear into bite-size pieces; wash and spin dry. Trim the stems of 1 bunch arugula. Shell ½ pound (225 g) English peas and cut ½ pound (225 g) sugar snap peas in half lengthwise.

MAKE THE EGG YOLK AND NUTRITIONAL YEAST LEMONY DRESSING: In a small bowl, combine the zest and juice of 1 lemon, 1 egg yolk, and ½ teaspoon mustard. Slowly add ½ cup (120 ml) oil, whisking constantly, until emulsified. Add 2 tablespoons chopped chives and a few pinches nutritional yeast and season with salt and pepper.

ASSEMBLE AND SERVE: Build the salad on a serving plate or platter starting with the lettuce, arugula, and 1 handful pea shoots. Scatter the English and sugar snap peas and mint leaves on top. Drizzle with the dressing. Sprinkle with pickled chive blossoms, 1 handful almonds, and just a pinch of red pepper flakes if desired.

peas and prosciut

Peas and crispy prosciutto on a cloud of homemade ricotta? Heaven on earth. It's completely okay to use frozen English peas here, which are sometimes sweeter than fresh peas, but take the time to make the ricotta—you won't regret it.

PRODUCE

1 pound (455 g) fresh English peas in their pods, or 1 cup (145 g) shelled fresh or frozen peas

1 pound (455 g) sugar snap peas

1 bunch scallions

1 lemon

1 handful fresh mint leaves

1 handful fresh dill, roughly chopped

DAIRY

1 cup (250 ml) Homemade Ricotta (page 259)

MEAT

¼ pound (115 g) finest prosciutto

PANTRY

Kosher salt and freshly ground black pepper

Extra-virgin olive oil

Flaky salt

PREP: In a small pot, bring heavily salted water to a boil, and prepare an ice bath with a fine-mesh sieve placed over it. Add 1 cup (145 g) shelled English peas and cook until tender and bright green, 2 to 4 minutes. Immediately transfer to the ice bath. Drain and dry off on a clean towel or paper towels. Transfer to a large bowl.

Remove the strings of 1 pound (455 g) sugar snap peas. Halve larger peas on the bias. Thinly slice 1 bunch scallions.

COOK: Heat a cast-iron skillet over high-ish heat. Add a glug of oil and once it is shimmering (not smoking) add the sugar snap peas. Give them a little toss so they get coated in oil and then let them sit for 2 minutes before touching them again—you want them to char! After 2 minutes, add the scallions and some kosher salt and pepper, and stir them around a bit for 2 to 4 more minutes (until they are crisp-tender). Zest 1 lemon into the pan, then squeeze juice from ½ lemon into the pan. Toss around a bit. Transfer to the bowl with the English peas and let cool.

Return the pan to the heat, giving a quick wipe if there are any scallion bits in there. Tear the ¼ pound (115 g) prosciutto into thin strips and add to the still-hot pan. Cook in batches until crispy, about 1 minute per batch.

ASSEMBLE AND SERVE: Spread 1 cup (250 ml) ricotta onto serving plates or a platter with the back of a spoon and season with kosher salt and pepper. Toss 1 handful mint and 1 handful dill with the peas and sprinkle them over the ricotta. Top with the crispy prosciutto and sprinkle with a bit of flaky salt.

grilled leeks mimosa redux

SERVES 2 TO 4 AS A STARTER OR SIDE

There are some dishes that are best enjoyed while sitting al fresco in Paris, drinking strong coffees and Champagne and smoking cigarettes at a late lunch. Like something so romantically French it's called mimosa because the grated eggs look like the small yellow flowers. Adapted for enjoying at home, this is not quite mimosa and not quite gribiche, the other, chunkier, French eggy vinaigrette, but whatever it is, it's delicious, no matter where on earth you are.

PRODUCE

8 young leeks

1 handful fresh parsley leaves

1 handful fresh dill, thick stems removed

1 lemon

DAIRY

4 large eggs

PANTRY

Kosher salt and freshly ground black pepper

Extra-virgin olive oil

2 teaspoons Champagne vinegar

1 tablespoon grainy mustard

3 tablespoons capers

PREP: Trim the ends off 8 leeks and peel off any dead-looking leaves. Trim the tops down so the leeks are 10 to 12 inches long, depending on the pan you plan on using. Cut in half lengthwise. Run each leek half under cold running water and make sure any dirt or sand is rinsed from the layers.

COOK: Hard-boil 4 eggs (see page 263). Cut each egg into quarters. Season with plenty of salt and pepper.

Fill a wide pot with a couple of inches of salted water. Bring to a boil, add the leeks, and cook until just tender when pierced with a knife, 3 to 4 minutes. Drain and transfer the leeks cut side down to paper towels. Pat them off and make sure they are completely dry.

The leeks can be charred either in a cast-iron skillet or on a grill. For skillet cooking, heat the skillet over high heat, add a good drizzle of oil, season well with salt and pepper, and cook, undisturbed, for 3 to 4 minutes, then turn and cook the other side. For the grill, heat to medium-high (about 425°F/220°C), brush the leeks with oil, season with salt and pepper, and grill until charred in places, 3 to 4 minutes per side.

MAKE THE CAPER VINAIGRETTE: In a small bowl, combine 2 teaspoons Champagne vinegar, 1 tablespoon mustard, and 3 tablespoons capers.

ASSEMBLE AND SERVE: Arrange the leeks on a serving plate or platter. Place the egg quarters on top. Toss 1 handful parsley and 1 handful dill with the dressing and spoon over the leeks. Season with a little extra pepper on top and a few lemon wedges on the side.

roasted little potatoes and radishes with chive butter

Radishes are always the first thing to grow in my garden. I love them mostly because they grow so fast, and they keep me entertained and hopeful until everything else begins to catch up. But also, they are delicious. Roasting them in really high-quality French butter mellows them a bit, sweetens them. Combined with little potatoes and flavorful chives, they become irresistible, elegant, and so much more than a humble side dish. Eat them for breakfast with a soft-boiled egg and a coffee with steamed milk.

PRODUCE

3 tablespoons finely chopped fresh chives

2 bunches radishes

1 pound (455 g) very little new potatoes

DAIRY

3 tablespoons really high-quality unsalted European butter, at room temperature

PANTRY

Kosher salt and freshly ground black pepper

Good crusty sourdough bread, for serving

MAKE THE CHIVE BUTTER: In a small-ish bowl, use a rubber spatula or a fork to make sure the 3 tablespoons butter is really room temperature (smooth and mixable). Mix in 3 tablespoons chopped chives until combined. Season with salt and pepper.

PREP: Trim the tops off 2 bunches radishes and cut large ones in half. Cut 1 pound (455 g) new potatoes into halves.

COOK: Preheat the oven to 425°F (220°C).

Put the radishes and potatoes in a cast-iron skillet or on a small rimmed baking sheet with the chive butter. Roast, shaking the pan once or twice, until deep golden brown in spots and the radishes are tender, about 25 to 30 minutes.

ASSEMBLE AND SERVE: Transfer to a serving platter, sprinkle with a little fresh pepper, and enjoy with some delicious crusty bread.

smoked trout, cucumber, and potatoes with crème fraîche dressing

Whatever your feelings about brunch are, this salad, to me, is the perfect excuse to have people over in the middle of the day and drink mimosas. It feels very fancy, but doesn't take much more time than toasting bagels. Smoked trout is a milder alternative to smoked salmon—but smoked salmon would be delicious as well.

PRODUCE

2 Persian cucumbers

1 pound (455 g) Peewee (or other very small) potatoes

1 lemon

2 tablespoons chopped fresh dill, plus more for serving

1 bunch arugula

1 bunch sorrel (or baby arugula)

DAIRY

2 tablespoons crème fraîche

MEAT

½ pound (225 g) smoked trout

French trout roe (optional)

PANTRY

Extra-virgin olive oil

Kosher salt and freshly ground black pepper

1 tablespoon grainy mustard

PREP: Preheat the oven to 425°F (220°C).

Slice 2 Persian cucumbers ¼ inch (6 mm) thick. Cut 1 pound (455 g) Peewee potatoes in half.

COOK: On a rimmed baking sheet, toss the potatoes with 2 glugs oil and season with salt and pepper. Arrange cut sides down on the baking sheet, and roast until the potatoes are tender and no longer stuck to the pan, about 25 minutes. They should be beautifully golden. Let cool almost to room temperature.

MAKE THE CRÈME FRAÎCHE DRESSING: In a large bowl, combine 2 tablespoons crème fraîche, 1 tablespoon mustard, and the zest and juice of 1 lemon. Season with salt and pepper.

ASSEMBLE AND SERVE: Add the roasted potatoes to the bowl with the dressing. Break the trout into bite-size pieces using a fork or your fingers and add to the bowl. Add the cucumbers. Add 2 tablespoons chopped dill and toss well to combine, checking for seasoning. Add 1 bunch arugula and 1 bunch sorrel to your serving plates or platters and gently add the trout mixture to top the greens. Sprinkle with more dill, and to make this dish really special, add a bit of French trout roe.

simple spring greens with frizzled shallots

A simple salad is often overlooked, left out of cookbooks and magazine articles because everyone already knows how to make that; it's been done before. But sometimes we need a reminder, a back-to-basics moment, a pause to remember that a homemade vinaigrette and some fresh greens is a beautiful and delicious dish.

PRODUCE

1 lemon

1 recipe Frizzled Shallots (page 261), plus ¼ cup (60 ml) reserved shallot oil

5 cups (200 g) baby lettuce mix

PANTRY

2 teaspoons Dijon mustard

½ teaspoon honey

Extra-virgin olive oil

Kosher salt and freshly ground black pepper

MAKE THE BASIC DIJON VINAIGRETTE: In a large bowl, combine 2 teaspoons mustard, ½ teaspoon honey, the zest of 1 lemon, and the juice of ½ lemon (about 2 tablespoons). While whisking, drizzle in ¼ cup (60 ml) reserved shallot oil, continuing to whisk until emulsified. Season with salt and pepper.

ASSEMBLE AND SERVE: Toss 5 cups (200 g) greens in the bowl with the dressing, transfer to individual bowls or plates or a serving bowl and sprinkle with the frizzled shallots. Season with a bit of fresh pepper.

spring lettuces, avocado, and creamy dressing

Capers are amazing. Frying them makes them even better because it adds a little crispy crunch to their saltiness, and they make this simple salad really, really good. I love the combination of crunchy lettuce, smooth avocado, and a creamy dressing. A handful of any fresh herb you have on hand, pepitas, or leftover protein, could be a great addition too.

PRODUCE

2 to 3 heads Little Gem lettuce

2 avocados

1 lemon

PANTRY

Extra-virgin olive oil

¼ cup (30 g) drained capers

Lemony Yogurt Vinaigrette (page 259)

COOK: Heat just less than ¼ inch (6 mm) oil in a small frying pan. Pat ¼ cup (30 g) capers dry on paper towels—make sure they are very dry before adding to the hot oil, or they will pop and splatter. Fry the capers for about 4 minutes, until beginning to get a little golden and crispy. Transfer to a paper towel–lined plate, and let drain for a minute.

PREP: Separate the leaves of 2 to 3 heads lettuce and tear into bite-size pieces; wash and spin dry. Halve, pit, peel, and slice 2 avocados and squeeze a bit of lemon juice over the slices to prevent them from browning.

ASSEMBLE AND SERVE: Arrange the lettuce on a serving platter and snuggle the avocado slices into the little pockets between the leaves. Drizzle with a bit of the vinaigrette and sprinkle with the capers. Serve with lemon wedges.

martha's mango and mozzarella with young lettuces

It was late one night at Martha's home after a long Thanksgiving shoot. The lighting was still all set up in the kitchen, so we maneuvered around it to make ourselves something to eat. My friend Molly and I made a lemony vinaigrette and washed young lettuces from the greenhouse while Martha sliced perfectly ripe mango and told us about the time she traveled around Morocco in a Volkswagen van. If you can find a few heads of young lettuce at the farmers' market, that would be best—otherwise just green leaf or butter lettuce will work fine.

PRODUCE

1 lemon

2 small, ripe mangoes (preferably Ataulfo)

2 small heads young lettuce, mixed varieties (8½ ounces/240 g)

DAIRY

1 ball (about 4 to 6 ounces/115 to 170 g) fresh mozzarella cheese, in water (yes, that kind, please!)

PANTRY

2 teaspoons Dijon mustard

4 teaspoons Champagne vinegar

1 teaspoon honey

¼ cup (60 ml) extra-virgin olive oil

Kosher salt and freshly ground black pepper

Flaky salt

MAKE THE LEMONY CHAMPAGNE VINAIGRETTE (WITH MUSTARD): In a large bowl, whisk together 2 teaspoons mustard, the zest and juice of 1 lemon, 4 teaspoons Champagne vinegar, and 1 teaspoon honey. While whisking, slowly drizzle in ¼ cup (60 ml) olive oil until emulsified. Season well with kosher salt and pepper.

PREP: Peel 2 mangoes using a Y-peeler. Hold a mango upright and find the tallest-looking side. The pit is long and flat and will run along that line, so start by cutting off both larger cheeks. Then, carefully running your knife along the curve of the pit, cut off the smaller side pieces. Thinly slice all of your mango.

Separate the leaves of 2 heads lettuce and tear into bite-size pieces to make about 6 cups (240 g); wash and spin dry. Thinly slice 1 ball mozzarella cheese.

ASSEMBLE AND SERVE: Toss your lettuce with about half of the dressing. Arrange on a serving plate or platter and then top with sliced mango and mozzarella—drizzle with more dressing as desired, and sprinkle with flaky salt.

simple egg salad with lots of dill

MAKES 2½ CUPS (555 G), OR ENOUGH FOR AT LEAST 4 TO 6 SANDWICHES

Egg salad is my best friend Glennis's favorite salad. She loves this version, and had no idea it was so easy to make at home. Stop buying it and start making it and keeping it in your fridge! She suggests eating it as a sandwich, as a lettuce wrap, and, because she's brilliant, as a dip for chips. You could stir in some finely chopped cornichon or capers if you have them on hand, but I like to keep it simple.

PRODUCE

1 stalk celery

¼ cup (13 g) chopped fresh dill (leave the thick stems behind), plus a few sprigs for garnish

Butter lettuce, Little Gem, or arugula leaves

Lemon wedges

Pickle-flavored chips, for serving (optional)

DAIRY

8 large eggs

PANTRY

1 tablespoon Dijon mustard

⅓ cup (75 ml) mayonnaise

Kosher salt and freshly ground black pepper

Pinch cayenne pepper

Toast or pickle-flavored potato chips (optional)

PREP: Finely chop 1 stalk celery.

MAKE THE DRESSING: In a large bowl, whisk together 1 tablespoon mustard, ⅓ cup (75 ml) mayonnaise, and the celery. Season with salt, pepper, and a pinch of cayenne. Whisk in ¼ cup (13 g) chopped dill.

COOK: Bring a medium pot of water to a boil. Prepare an ice bath. Gently lower 8 eggs into the water. Lower the heat a bit if the eggs are bouncing around like crazy. Cook them for 13 minutes, then transfer immediately to the ice bath. Let them cool completely.

Peel the eggs and make space for chopping them. Quarter the eggs, discarding the whites of two of the eggs, then roughly chop. Add them to the bowl with the dressing as you go. Combine and mash with a whisk.

ASSEMBLE AND SERVE: Serve on toast with lettuce and a wedge of lemon on the side and a few sprigs of dill on top. Or just dip some pickle-flavored chips in there and forget your life.

salade niçoise

SERVES 2 TO 4 AS A MEAL

I really believe that sometimes it's best not to mess too much with a classic, especially one like a Niçoise salad. But a few handfuls of herbs at the end really gives this salad so much more flavor and freshness.

PRODUCE

½ pound (225 g) green beans, preferably haricots verts

½ small shallot

1 pint (280 g) cherry tomatoes

1 head Little Gem lettuce

½ pound (225 g) baby potatoes

1 lemon

Fresh basil, parsley, and dill, for serving

DAIRY

2 large eggs

PANTRY

Kosher salt and freshly ground black pepper

2 tablespoons sherry vinegar

1 tablespoon grainy mustard

¼ cup (60 ml) extra-virgin olive oil

1 cup (155 g) olives, preferably Niçoise, or a mix

½ cup (70 g) caperberries

1 (6.7-ounce/190 g) jar pole-caught tuna packed in oil, drained

PREP: Snip the tops from ½ pound (225 g) green beans. Finely chop ½ shallot. Cut 1 pint (280 g) cherry tomatoes in half. Separate the leaves of 1 head lettuce and tear into bite-size pieces; wash and spin dry.

COOK: Prepare an ice bath. Put ½ pound (225 g) baby potatoes in a medium pot and cover with cold water by about 2 inches (5 cm). Bring to a boil and boil for about 12 minutes, until the potatoes can be easily pierced with a knife. Scoop the potatoes out with a spider and set aside to cool.

Add a good amount of salt to the water and bring to a boil again. Add the green beans and cook until bright green and crisp tender, about 2 minutes. Transfer with the spider or tongs to the ice bath. Add 2 eggs to the water and cook for 10 minutes, then place in the ice bath to cool. Transfer the green beans to a paper towel to dry. Peel the eggs and cut into quarters and set aside for the moment.

MAKE THE CLASSIC SHERRY VINAIGRETTE: Put the shallot in a small bowl. Whisk in 2 tablespoons sherry vinegar, 1 tablespoon mustard, and the juice of ½ lemon. While whisking, drizzle in ¼ cup (60 ml) oil. Whisk until emulsified. Season with salt and pepper.

ASSEMBLE AND SERVE: Begin by putting the lettuce leaves in a large bowl, drizzling in a bit of the dressing, seasoning with salt and pepper, tossing, and arranging on a serving platter. Continue to dress each element of the salad one at a time: potatoes, beans, tomatoes, 1 cup (155 g) olives, ½ cup (70 g) caperberries, and the tuna. Take care to do so lightly—the salad shouldn't be drenched in vinaigrette. As you dress each element, arrange it in a cluster on top of the lettuce. The eggs can be arranged in various places on the platter, snuggled into the other vegetables. Scatter basil, parsley, and dill all over and then serve with the remaining ½ lemon cut into wedges.

matzo fattoush

This is a great dish to serve as part of a Passover meal, and an even better way to use up the couple of extra leftover matzo in an opened box that are a little on the stale side (after you've also saved some to make your matzo brei—custardy matzo and eggs, one of my all-time favorite breakfasts).

PRODUCE

1 lemon

½ small red onion

5 Persian cucumbers, or 1 English cucumber

2 pints (565 g) cherry tomatoes

1 handful chopped fresh dill

1 handful fresh parsley leaves

1 handful fresh mint leaves

DAIRY

1 large egg

PANTRY

1 tablespoon pomegranate molasses

¼ cup (60 ml) extra-virgin olive oil

Kosher salt and freshly ground black pepper

3 matzo

3 tablespoons store-bought Everything Seasoning or za'atar

Ground sumac

Preheat the oven to 350°F (175°C).

MAKE THE POMEGRANATE MOLASSES VINAIGRETTE: In a small bowl, whisk together the juice of 1 lemon, 1 tablespoon pomegranate molasses, and ¼ cup (60 ml) olive oil and season well with salt and pepper.

COOK: Set 3 matzo on a rimmed baking sheet. Beat 1 egg with a fork until blended. Brush the matzo on both sides with egg and sprinkle 3 tablespoons Everything Seasoning on both sides. Bake, flipping once, until golden on both sides and crispy, about 15 minutes total.

PREP: Thinly slice ½ red onion and 5 Persian or 1 English cucumber. Cut 2 pints (565 g) cherry tomatoes in half.

ASSEMBLE AND SERVE: Break the matzo into bite-size pieces and put in a large bowl. Add the onion, cucumbers, and tomatoes. Add 1 handful each of dill, parsley, and mint. Pour the dressing into the bowl and toss everything to combine. Sprinkle with sumac and season again with salt and pepper if necessary. Transfer to a serving platter or bowl and sprinkle with a bit of additional sumac.

tokyo turnips with miso mayo

SERVES 4 · AS A STARTER OR SIDE

I made these turnips for my friend Benny and he called the next morning to say he dreamed about them that night. Now he makes them all the time and I'm very tickled by all of that. Tokyo turnips are tender little babies with a beautiful sharp bite. I've included two options for how to serve them: I love the way they look raw—it makes for an elegant and surprising presentation—but roasting mellows the flavor and makes the whole thing just kind of melt in your mouth, especially when paired with this creamy dressing. The umami/sweetness/funk of the miso really adds a little something special to the mayonnaise.

PRODUCE

5 scallions, white parts only, greens reserved for another use

1 bunch Tokyo turnips (about 5 small), tops reserved for another use

PANTRY

¼ cup (60 ml) mayonnaise (preferably Kewpie)

1 teaspoon white miso

Kosher salt

Toasted sesame oil

1 tablespoon toasted sesame seeds

1 to 2 tablespoons neutral oil (for roasted turnips)

PREP: Thinly slice the white parts of 5 scallions.

If you are making the raw turnips, make an ice bath in a medium bowl. Thinly slice the turnips on a mandoline right into the ice bath. Let sit for about 20 minutes while you prep the rest.

If you are roasting the turnips, halve or quarter them, depending on their size.

MAKE THE CREAMY MISO DRESSING: In a little bowl, combine ¼ cup (60 ml) mayonnaise and 1 teaspoon miso. I like to use a rubber spatula to kind of smooth them into each other, but warming the miso for a few seconds in the microwave makes it a bit easier to combine. Check for seasoning and see if you need a bit of salt.

ASSEMBLE AND SERVE (IF USING RAW TURNIPS): Make sure you drain and dry the turnips really, really well on clean towels or paper towels or in a salad spinner before you plate the dish. Spread a thin layer of the dressing on the bottom of a plate and arrange sliced turnips on top. Drizzle with sesame oil. Sprinkle with the scallion whites, and sesame seeds. Serve immediately as the turnips can start to get a little liquidy if they sit for a while.

COOK (IF MAKING ROASTED TURNIPS): Preheat the oven to 425°F (220°C).

Put the turnips on a rimmed baking sheet, toss with 1 to 2 tablespoons neutral oil, and season with salt. Roast until the turnips are tender and browned in spots, about 25 minutes. Serve warm or room temperature over the miso mayo dressing with scallions, sesame oil, and sesame seeds.

summer

It's July, it's summer. It's hot and the nights are long, and it's the time of the year when you can get lucky with evenings that hold a certain kind of magic, the way a certain song can, the way it can linger in your mind, when you can really feel it. Did you dream it? Sometimes the only proof is the sand at the bottom of your bedsheets.

A few Julys ago, I moved into a loft. It had its own unique tropical climate. It was a hot box of stale skunky weed smoke and sweat in Bed-Stuy, a sauna with a few tired AC units drooping out of the windows. I begged, and friends came, clothes sticking to their bodies. One of the first nights after I moved in, we stood around the kitchen counter with a loaf of sourdough, some Kewpie mayo, flaky salt, and a bunch of fat juicy heirloom tomatoes. We made sandwiches until the bread was gone—my friends' son Leroy was holding the bread with two hands, mashing it into his face to lick off the mayo by the end. We washed it down with really cold natural white wine. I cooked so much in that apartment, I had so many parties, but it is always the spontaneous tomato sandwich night I'll think about. There is always a little piece of me clinging to that place, that time, that feeling.

There are so many things to love about summer . . . Wiping the fuzz from a sun-ripened peach, letting its juice run down your hand, your arm, your face. Cherries staining your lips and pits all over the counter, the table, in bowls. Round little sour cherries so bright you can't believe they are real. Ice-cold melon balls, any kind really— sweet, musky melons, slick and smooth, quenching your thirst and making you salivate. The way it feels to be completely full of melon. The way it feels to be completely sticky all over from ripe fruit. Eating anything that has just come off of a bed of crushed ice. The crispness, the snap of a cucumber. A Sungold tomato bursting in your mouth. Slicing a delicate tomato, swollen, and ready to split open out of its skin, and smelling that clean, fresh, earthy, tangy scent.

How do you hold on to that feeling?

rhubarb and strawberries with toasted buckwheat and salted honeycomb

Every summer, when strawberries are finally at their peak (sweet, and red all the way through), I make a big batch of strawberry rhubarb and ginger jam. I love how tart raw rhubarb is—and with bright-red-on-the-inside strawberries, you really don't need all that sugar that goes in jam to enjoy these flavors, which feel a bit unusual. Buckwheat is part of the same plant family as rhubarb, and its toasty nuttiness is heaven when they are combined.

PREP: Julienne or very thinly slice 4 stalks rhubarb and cut 1 quart (580 g) strawberries into slices (or halves, if they're small).

In a large bowl, combine the rhubarb, strawberries, and 2 teaspoons honey. Squeeze in just a little bit of lemon juice, a teaspoon or so. Use a Microplane to grate 1 inch (2.5 cm) ginger into the bowl. Let this sit for at least 10 minutes.

ASSEMBLE AND SERVE: On a large serving plate or platter, spoon the strawberry mixture over 1 cup (240 ml) ricotta or yogurt and sprinkle with ¼ cup (40 g) buckwheat. Add the honeycomb, if you have it, and a good sprinkle of flaky salt.

STYLING TIP

Using a julienne peeler to create long ribbons of rhubarb is an unexpected and visually striking way to plate this dish, and it gives it a lot of volume. I prefer this to thinly slicing or shaving with a Y-peeler or mandoline because the julienne ribbons don't go limp—they keep a little bit of texture even when sitting.

PRODUCE

4 stalks rhubarb

1 quart (580 g) the sweetest strawberries

1 teaspoon fresh lemon juice, or to taste

1 (1-inch/2.5 cm) piece ginger, peeled

DAIRY

1 cup (240 ml) Homemade Ricotta (page 259), or thick yogurt

PANTRY

2 teaspoons honey

¼ cup (40 g) toasted buckwheat groats (kasha)

A few thin slices honeycomb (optional)

Flaky sea salt

strawberries, rose, and sumac

This is the most romantic breakfast one could possibly have or make for someone else. Forget misshapen pancakes that make a huge mess and never come out quite right, and aren't you sick of avocado toast and scrambled eggs? I want to eat this in bed with the ripest, sweetest little strawberries, delicate rose petals, creamy yogurt scented with orange, plump dates, and a strong latte.

PREP: In a small bowl, combine 1 cup (240 ml) yogurt and 6 chopped dates. Use a fork or rubber spatula to sort of mash the dates into the yogurt the best you can. Use a Microplane to grate the zest of 1 orange into the bowl, and squeeze a couple of tablespoons of its juice in. Add ¼ teaspoon rosewater and mix.

Hull and slice 1 quart (580 g) strawberries.

ASSEMBLE AND SERVE: Spread the yogurt mixture on the bottom of two shallow bowls or plates. Scatter strawberries on top, and rose petals on top of the strawberries. Sprinkle with a bit of sumac and 1 handful mint leaves.

PRODUCE

1 orange

1 quart (580 g) strawberries

Petals from 1 rose (organic, not sprayed; ask at the farmers' market or pick from your yard— not from the bodega or florist, please)

1 handful fresh mint leaves

DAIRY

1 cup (240 ml) plain unsweetened yogurt

PANTRY

6 very soft plump Medjool or Barhi dates, pitted and finely chopped

¼ teaspoon rosewater

Ground sumac

simply tomatoes and nasturtiums

Tomatoes in the height of summer don't need anything else to make them more delicious, but a few bright nasturtium petals fresh from the garden scattered on top makes this simple salad a breathtaking dish, for a special occasion or just a Tuesday night. The peppery bite from the nasturtium blossoms adds a subtle something, but not too much!

ASSEMBLE AND SERVE: Slice 1½ pounds (680 g) large heirloom tomatoes about ¼ inch (6 mm) thick and arrange on a serving platter. Next cut 1 pint (280 g) cherry tomatoes in half and add them to the platter. Drizzle with olive oil and sprinkle with salt, and then tear the petals off of some of the nasturtiums and leave others whole and scatter them over the tomatoes.

PRODUCE

1½ pounds (680 g) heirloom tomatoes in a variety of colors (about 5 large)

1 pint (280 g) cherry tomatoes

6 or so nasturtium blossoms (organic, not sprayed; ask at the farmers' market or pick from your yard—not from the bodega or florist, please)

PANTRY

Good extra-virgin olive oil

Flaky salt

california wedge

There are diehard fans of the wedge salad, and I get it, but I'm usually just not one of them. I like the idea, I like the look of it, but I can't remember the last time I went to a steakhouse. This wedge has what appeals to me about a wedge—the somehow quenching crispness that is only offered by iceberg lettuce, smoky, extra-crispy bacon, sweet little bursting cherry tomatoes. But I prefer the salty tang of French feta cheese, and a fresh green herbaceous dressing that begs to be eaten al fresco at home, far from the rich blue cheese dressings and dark, table-clothed interiors of Midtown Manhattan.

PREP: Give 1 head iceberg lettuce a good rinse under cold water, then pat dry. Remove any leaves that seem dirty or wilted. Trim the end of the iceberg just a little bit, and peel off any damaged or not-so-hot-looking outer leaves. Cut in half root to tip, then cut in half roof to tip again. Place each wedge on its own plate or put them all on a platter. Cut 1 pint (280 g) cherry tomatoes in half.

ASSEMBLE AND SERVE: Spoon a bit of the dressing over the top of each wedge. Scatter the tomatoes on the top and over the sides—some will stick to the sides but it's okay if they spill off onto the plate. Crumble 3 ounces (85 g) feta over the top, crumble 1 pound (455 g) cooked bacon (precooked weight) over the top, and sprinkle it with lots of mint, basil, and dill. Top with a pinch of pepper.

PRODUCE

1 head iceberg lettuce

1 pint (280 g) cherry tomatoes, preferably Sungold

1 handful fresh mint leaves

1 handful fresh basil leaves

1 handful fresh dill, thick stems removed

DAIRY

1 recipe Green Goddess Dressing (page 262)

3 ounces (85 g) feta cheese (Valbreso or French)

MEAT

1 pound (455 g) bacon, cooked Snoop-style (page 260)

PANTRY

Freshly ground black pepper

yellow gazpacho

Even though gazpacho is really the salad of soups, I've never really been sure of it, or of any chilled soup, to be honest. I remember making gazpacho in elementary school in Spanish class, and looking around the room at people spooning it up, thinking, doesn't anyone else realize this is just salsa? But the addition of juicy little Sungold cherry tomatoes changed my mind. Here is my silky smooth, slightly sweet, just a little spicy yellow version—it gives me heartburn, but I can honestly say it's worth it. Make it a day in advance and the flavors will really meld.

PRODUCE

1 pound (455 g) yellow or orange tomatoes, cut into chunks, remove some of the seeds if you can

1 yellow bell pepper, seeds and ribs removed, chopped

1 English cucumber, peeled, seeds scooped out with a spoon

1 pound (455 g) Sungold cherry tomatoes

½ jalapeño (I keep the seeds in)

1 clove garlic

PANTRY

½ cup (120 ml) extra-virgin olive oil, plus more for serving (use something good here, bright, fruity, and fresh)

2 teaspoons kosher salt

2 teaspoons sherry vinegar

Freshly ground black pepper

PREP: Cut 1 pound (455 g) yellow tomatoes into chunks and remove some of the seeds if you can. Seed and chop 1 yellow bell pepper, removing the ribs. Peel 1 English cucumber and scoop out the seeds with a spoon.

For this smoothie-style gazpacho, just put everything but the sherry vinegar in the blender at once and blend until smooth. If you're using a smaller blender, you may have to work in batches. Once smooth, strain the soup though a fine-mesh sieve into a storage container with a lid. Depending on the ripeness of your tomatoes, I've found sometimes I have to add a couple of tablespoons of water to thin out the soup a bit—but peak-season tomatoes should be just fine! Add 2 teaspoons sherry vinegar, stir to combine, and refrigerate for at least 6 hours before tasting again for seasoning— you may have to add more salt and more vinegar to taste.

SERVE: Spoon into serving bowls and swirl with a little good olive oil and a bit of freshly ground black pepper.

pickled blackberry and shallot panzanella with sumac

I discovered blackberries in the brush around the house upstate where I lived for a summer and spent an entire day getting scratched and stained while picking these not-very-good, very seedy little blackberries. I picked too many and my fridge was already full of jam, so someone sent me an Olia Hercules recipe for tomato and blackberry salad as inspiration. If there are mulberries at your market, which are gone in the blink of an eye, this is a wonderful place to try them in place of blackberries.

PREP: Preheat the oven to 425°F (220°C).

In a large bowl, whisk together ¼ cup (60 ml) cider vinegar and 1 teaspoon honey. Thinly slice 1 shallot into rounds, cut 2 pints (560 g) cherry tomatoes in half, and add them, along with 1 pint (280 g) blackberries, to the bowl. Sprinkle with salt and let sit for about 15 minutes while the oven preheats—don't touch it or mix it! You want the shallots to get the majority of the vinegar, but you want the blackberries to get a little bit, and you want the tomato juices to start to leak into the liquid.

PRODUCE

1 shallot

2 pints (560 g) cherry tomatoes

1 pint (280 g) blackberries (or mulberries if you can find them!)

1 handful fresh basil (any variety, but something purplish is extra beautiful)

PANTRY

¼ cup (60 ml) cider vinegar

1 teaspoon honey

Kosher salt

4 slices sourdough bread (can be a couple days old, doesn't matter!), cut into 1-inch (2.5 cm) cubes

Extra-virgin olive oil

Ground sumac

COOK: On a baking sheet, toss the bread cubes with a few glugs of oil and a sprinkle of salt. Toast, tossing once, until golden brown, 8 to 10 minutes.

ASSEMBLE AND SERVE: When you're just about ready to serve, *gently* toss the bread and some basil into the tomato mixture. Be careful, because if the blackberries burst, it's not the worst thing, but it gets a little messy looking. Top with more basil and a sprinkle of salt. Sprinkle with sumac.

STYLING TIP
This salad looks better plated on a platter than it does in a bowl, so I like to transfer it from the large mixing bowl before serving.

plum, tomato, burrata, chile, and cilantro

SERVES 4 AS A STARTER OR SIDE (PAIRS PERFECTLY WITH ANYTHING GRILLED)

For all that talk about how tomatoes need absolutely nothing to make them delicious, I still can't resist mixing them with a few things that make them even better. Spicy, sweet, and bold—this is a salad with complementary flavors that make each ingredient sing. The creamy burrata makes each bite luscious.

PRODUCE

1 small red onion

2 pints (560 g) Sungold cherry tomatoes

6 plums (Santa Rosa or black plums are best—pluots work too)

1 Fresno chile

A handful of the most beautiful fresh cilantro leaves, and flowers if you have them

DAIRY

2 balls burrata (approximately 8 ounces/225 g total)

PANTRY

½ cup (120 ml) red wine vinegar

A touch of honey

Kosher salt and freshly ground black pepper

Extra-virgin olive oil

PREP: Very thinly slice 1 red onion on a mandoline. Put it in a small bowl, add ½ cup (120 ml) red wine vinegar, a touch of honey, and a pinch of salt and pepper. Let sit while you finish prepping.

Cut 2 pints (560 g) cherry tomatoes in half, and thinly slice 6 plums. If you can pit the plums neatly, good for you. I usually cut off the cheeks and then try to make even, thin slices from them, snacking on whatever doesn't look perfect. Thinly slice 1 chile on the mandoline.

ASSEMBLE AND SERVE: On a large serving platter, arrange the tomatoes and plums. Scatter the onions and most of their liquid onto the platter, but don't drown everything! Tear 2 balls burrata into bite-size pieces and arrange over the platter—each person should be able to get a nice chunk without fussing or making a mess. Sprinkle with the chile and warn people who are sensitive to heat that it's spicy. Drizzle with oil, sprinkle with 1 handful cilantro, and season with salt and pepper.

Ode to the Scuttlebutt
(page 148)

ode to the scuttlebutt

A little hole in my heart remains for where Saltie once stood—a tiny box wedged between other storefronts, a few items on the menu, simple combinations. Simple sandwiches really, but so good.

The Scuttlebutt was a tangy, salty, chewy, herbaceous, perfect sandwich. The first wave of saltiness—capers, olives, creamy feta—was met by the sweetness of the pickled beets, the richness of the egg yolk and the aioli, and the freshness of the tangle of herbs all between two spongy pillows of just-out-of-the-oven focaccia.

The first time I had the Scuttlebutt I took my friend Penny to the Rockaways. Surrounded by all the bodies and tattoos and conversations that a city beach supplies, we ate our Scuttlebutts in the bright sunshine on the shore, while washing them down with an ice-cold rosé. We had to jump in the water when we were done because the feta had crumbled, and the capers had scattered, and the herbs had stuck to our sunscreen. It was the perfect day, and the Scuttlebutt really was the perfect sandwich—and this panzanella is not quite as good as that, but it satisfies my cravings, and is a bit more manageable in a bowl.

You can use store-bought focaccia, but it's easy to make at home and couldn't be more delicious. You can also buy good-quality pickled beets at the store or farmers' market if you don't have time to prep them yourself. This is a great way to use up day-old focaccia if you can keep it in your house for that long. Make the pickles and the focaccia two days in advance if you're going to make them. Really. You can make the aioli too and toast the bread in advance.

PRODUCE

4 small beets, roasted according to instructions on page 263

½ small red onion, sliced

1 pint (280 g) cherry tomatoes

1 lemon

1 cup (30 g) fresh mint leaves

1 cup (30 g) fresh dill, thick stems removed

1 cup (30 g) fresh parsley leaves

DAIRY

6 ounces (170 g) feta cheese (Valbreso or French), thinly sliced

4 hard-boiled eggs (see page 263), peeled and quartered

1 cup (240 ml) red wine vinegar

1 tablespoon sugar

2 teaspoons black peppercorns

2 teaspoons coriander seeds

1 bay leaf

⅓ cup (75 ml) mayonnaise

1 teaspoon smoked paprika

Kosher salt and freshly ground black pepper

Foccacia Bread (page 258), torn into 1-inch (2.5 cm) pieces (6 cups/430 g)

¼ cup (45 g) pitted cured black olives

3 tablespoons capers

Extra-virgin olive oil

PREP: Let the roasted beets cool until you can handle them safely, then rub the skins off with a paper towel—this removes the skins easily and keeps your hands kind of clean (you can also wear gloves). Slice just under ¼ inch (6 mm) thick and place in a pint jar or small container, along with the sliced onion.

In a small saucepan, bring to a boil 1 cup (240 ml) red wine vinegar, 1 cup (240 ml) water, 1 tablespoon sugar, 1 teaspoon peppercorns, 1 teaspoon coriander seeds, and 1 bay leaf. Pour the liquid into the container with the beets and onion, and refrigerate for at least 2 days or up to 1 month. (Multiply the recipe if you'd like to make extra while you're at it!)

Stir together ⅓ cup (75 ml) mayonnaise and 1 teaspoon smoked paprika and season with salt. That's your aioli.

Cut 1 (280 g) pint cherry tomatoes in half.

COOK: Preheat the oven to 425°F (220°C). Put 6 cups (430 g) torn focaccia on a rimmed baking sheet and toast for about 10 minutes, until a bit crunchy and golden. Set aside to cool.

ASSEMBLE AND SERVE: In a large bowl, combine the tomatoes, 4 sliced pickled beets and some of the onion and about 3 tablespoons of the pickling liquid (you may need a bit more, if the salad looks dry), ¼ cup (45 g) olives, 3 tablespoons capers, the juice of ½ lemon, and a bit of olive oil. Combine and add the cooled bread and mix it around and let it soak up all the juices for a few minutes.

Toss in the mint, dill, and parsley leaves and add a drizzle of olive oil and a little salt and pepper.

When ready to eat, smear the aioli on your serving platters or plates and pile up the salad. Arrange 6 ounces (170 g) sliced feta and 4 quartered hard-boiled eggs on top.

blt potato salad

SERVES 6 TO 8 AS A SIDE

By the middle of July, I start eating a BLT almost every day, and each time I am reminded that it's the perfect sandwich. Crispy, salty bacon, and crunchy lettuce. But the big slices of fat, juicy tomatoes, seeping, mixing in with the fat of mayonnaise—that is what I'm addicted to. My friend Steve in Bovina grows the best tomatoes I've ever had, tomatoes that are bursting with flavor and begging to be sprinkled with a bit of flaky salt. These are the kind of tomatoes, so plump and ripe, that just the memory of them can keep you going through the winter— perhaps they've somehow stored the warmth of the sunshine inside you. Since it's no guarantee that even peak heirloom tomatoes somewhere else may be even half as good as Steve's, I've used cherry tomatoes here, because those little guys are so plentiful in the summer months and delicious no matter who's growing them and hold up a bit better if you're traveling to a picnic or barbecue. This is the perfect way to share the feeling of a BLT with a group, or a wonderful excuse to eat more than one combination of bacon, lettuce, and tomatoes in a single day.

PRODUCE

1½ pounds (680 g) baby Yukon gold potatoes

2 cloves garlic

1 lemon

2 heads Little Gem lettuce

1 pint (280 g) cherry tomatoes

4 scallions

¼ cup (11 g) chopped fresh chives

MEAT

1 pound (455 g) bacon, cooked Snoop-style (page 260)

PANTRY

¼ cup (60 ml) mayonnaise

Kosher salt and freshly ground black pepper

Extra-virgin olive oil

Flaky salt

COOK: Put 1½ pounds (680 g) baby potatoes in a large pot and cover with water. Bring to a boil. Cook until easily pierced with a knife, about 12 minutes. Drain and spread out on a baking sheet to cool. Once cooled, consider slicing them—I think they are a bit easier to eat when cut in half, but if your potatoes are small enough, this might not be necessary.

PREP: Use a Microplane to grate 2 cloves garlic into a large bowl. Add the zest of 1 lemon, mix together, then stir in ¼ cup (60 ml) mayonnaise and season with salt and pepper. Add the potatoes to the bowl and toss.

MAKE THE LEMON VINAIGRETTE: In a small bowl, combine the juice of ½ lemon with a couple tablespoons oil. Season with salt and pepper.

ASSEMBLE AND SERVE: Separate the leaves of 2 heads lettuce and tear them into bite-size pieces; wash and spin dry. Put the lettuce in a large bowl and add a bit of the dressing to lightly coat and arrange on the serving platter. Scatter the potatoes on top of the lettuce. Cut 1 pint (280 g) cherry tomatoes in half and slice 4 scallions, and add them, along with the chives, to the bowl you used to dress the lettuce. Add the rest of the dressing, toss, and scatter this mixture on top of the potatoes. Crumble 1 pound (455 g) cooked bacon (precooked weight) on top. Sprinkle with a bit of flaky salt and some more pepper.

hugh's sungold and saffron panzanella

SERVES 6 AS A STARTER OR SIDE (EXCELLENT WITH GRILLED SEAFOOD OR CHICKEN)

A good panzanella is hard to find, and a good friend like Hugh is even harder to find. The perfect panzanella needs sweetness and acidity and the right amount of juice; it needs cubes of tangy sourdough bread that won't choke you. It needs bite—and I like something that brings a little surprise. A great Panzanella is a trust-worthy go-to for any summer get-together. I can't make a Panzanella without thinking about Hugh, who loves them, and making him his own Panzanella full of all of his favorite things is the least I can do, really.

PRODUCE

1 clove garlic

4 large yellow and orange heirloom tomatoes

1 pint (280 g) Sungold cherry tomatoes

¼ cup (11 g) chopped fresh chives

1 handful fresh basil leaves

1 handful chopped bronze fennel, or fennel fronds

PANTRY

½ boule sourdough bread (sesame bread is the best if you can find it!)

½ cup (60 g) thinly sliced pepperoncini

¼ cup (60 ml) white balsamic vinegar

Big pinch saffron

Kosher salt and freshly ground black pepper

¼ cup (60 ml) extra-virgin olive oil

COOK: Preheat the oven to 350°F (175°C).

Cut ½ boule bread into 1-inch-thick (2.5 cm) slices and toast on a baking sheet for 10 minutes. Remove from the oven and carefully rub the garlic clove over the toasted side of bread. Tear the bread into 1-inch (2.5 cm) pieces (you should have about 5 cups/250 g). Return to the oven and bake until just golden, about 5 more minutes. Let cool.

PREP AND MAKE THE SAFFRON VINAIGRETTE: Cut 4 heirloom tomatoes into wedges and cut 1 pint (280 g) cherry tomatoes in half. In a bowl, toss the tomatoes with ½ cup (60 g) thinly sliced pepperoncini, ¼ cup (60 ml) white balsamic vinegar, and a big pinch of saffron and season with salt and pepper. Mix well (I usually just do this with clean hands to really toss everything). Let sit for a few minutes for the saffron to bloom. Add ¼ cup (60 ml) oil, and let this mixture sit for at least 30 minutes or up to a few hours at room temperature. The longer it sits the more the tomato juice and other flavors will meld and the more delicious it will be.

ASSEMBLE AND SERVE: Toss the bread, tomato mixture, ¼ cup (11 g) chopped chives, 1 handful basil, and 1 handful chopped bronze fennel to combine. Don't do this in advance or the bread will get too mushy.

tortellini antipasto pasta salad

SERVES 10 TO 12 AS A SIDE

I would like to have an origin story set in the French countryside, or a medieval town outside of Tuscany with an ancient little grandmother who spoke no English who taught me everything she knew. I would have liked to have grown up spending summers by the shore somewhere in Spain, drinking fine wine since I could hold a stemmed glass. Even somewhere along the California coast would do, where fish jumped out of the sea into my lap, where I would run through my orchard and fill my baskets with lemons every morning.

But that's not how I grew up, nor is it how many of us really live. The most beautiful heirloom produce from the farmers' market is special and a luxury for when we have the time and access to that, which is not all the time. This is a salad I grew up eating. My mom made it in the summers with Italian dressing out of the bottle and diced raw peppers while I popped black olives onto my fingers and picked basil on the back porch. Most things come from the grocery store or cans or jars, and that is okay. Bring it to a barbecue and everyone will be really, really happy, choosing it over that fancy dish right next to it every time.

PRODUCE

2 cloves garlic

2 teaspoons fresh oregano, chopped

2 pints (560 g) cherry tomatoes, halved

2 lemons

2 cups (60 g) fresh parsley leaves

2 cups (60 g) fresh basil leaves

MEAT

¼ pound (115 g) Genoa salami, thinly sliced and cut into matchsticks

2 ounces (55 g) Calabrese salami (or spicy pepperoni), thinly sliced and halved

DAIRY

2 (10-ounce/280 g) bags cheese tortellini

1 cup (225 g) fresh bocconcini mozzarella, halved

¼ pound (115 g) provolone cheese, thinly sliced and cut into matchsticks

PANTRY

Kosher salt and freshly ground black pepper

2 tablespoons red wine vinegar

Pinch crushed red pepper flakes

¼ cup (60 ml) extra-virgin olive oil

½ cup (55 g) sliced pepperoncini peppers

½ cup (125 g) chopped grilled artichokes in oil

⅓ cup (45 g) sliced black olives

⅓ cup (45 g) sliced green olives

Get a big pot of salted water boiling.

MAKE THE HOMEMADE ITALIAN DRESSING:
Grate 2 cloves garlic into a large bowl, add
2 teaspoons chopped oregano, 2 tablespoons red
wine vinegar, the juice of ½ lemon, a pinch of red
pepper flakes, and ¼ cup (60 ml) oil and whisk to
combine; you'll toss everything else in here later.

COOK: Add 2 bags tortellini to the boiling
water and cook according to the package
instructions (it's usually about 3 minutes for
fresh/refrigerated pasta). Drain and set aside
to cool.

PREP: Cut 2 pints (560 g) cherry tomatoes
in half.

ASSEMBLE AND SERVE: Once it's cool, add
the tortellini to the dressing, along with the
tomatoes, 1 cup (225 g) bocconcini (cut in
half), ¼ pound (115 g) julienned provolone,
¼ pound (115 g) julienned Genoa salami,
2 ounces thinly sliced and halved Calabrese
salami, ½ cup (55 g) sliced pepperoncini,
½ cup (125 g) chopped grilled artichokes,
⅓ cup (45 g) sliced black olives, and ⅓ cup
(45 g) sliced green olives. Zest 1 lemon into
the bowl and toss everything to combine. If
you're serving right away, toss in 2 cups each of
parsley and basil; if you're not, wait—toss them
in right before serving to keep them looking
fresh and beautiful. Serve with lemon wedges.

snoop's bbq chicken cobb salad with all the good stuff

Over the last few years, I have been creeping in the background of Martha and Snoop Dogg's amazing friendship— and I just love Snoop. He has an amazing open attitude about cooking and always asks Martha to "teach me how to learn"—but I've learned a lot from Snoop too. I credit myself for giving him his first homemade crouton, but he showed me how to make the crispiest bacon ever (read more on page 260). He asked me to make him a recipe for a barbecue chicken Cobb salad with all the good stuff in it. It was 100 percent Snoop's idea to add the homemade blue corn tortilla strips, which was brilliant—it's exactly what a Cobb salad needs to tie everything together.

PRODUCE

3 heads Little Gem lettuce

1 pint (280 g) cherry tomatoes

1 avocado

2 Persian cucumbers

Fresh chives

MEAT

2 boneless, skinless chicken breasts (about 8 ounces/225 g each)

½ pound bacon, cooked Snoop-style (page 260)

DAIRY

2 to 4 large eggs

2 ounces (55 g) blue cheese

1 recipe Garlicky Buttermilk Ranch Dressing (page 259)

PANTRY

2 teaspoons Lawry's Seasoning Salt

½ teaspoon garlic powder

½ teaspoon chili powder

¼ teaspoon cayenne pepper

Freshly ground black pepper

1 cup (240 ml) Sweet Baby Ray's barbecue sauce

Neutral oil, for frying

4 small corn tortillas (blue if you can find them; store-bought strips are also fine!)

Kosher salt

MAKE THE RUB: In a small bowl, mix together 2 teaspoons Lawry's, ½ teaspoon garlic powder, ½ teaspoon chili powder, ¼ teaspoon cayenne, and ¼ teaspoon black pepper.

Coat the chicken breasts with the rub and let them sit for 15 minutes or, refrigerated, up to overnight.

COOK: Preheat the oven to 400°F (205°C). Get a medium pot of water boiling. Prepare an ice bath.

Place the coated chicken breasts on a parchment-lined rimmed baking sheet, and with a silicone brush, coat the chicken with barbecue sauce. Bake for 25 to 30 minutes, until the chicken reaches 165°F (74°C) on an instant-read thermometer.

Meanwhile, add 2 to 4 eggs to the boiling water. Cook for 10 minutes. Transfer to the ice bath. Wipe out and dry the saucepan completely; you'll use it to fry your tortilla strips.

Add ½ inch (12 mm) oil to the saucepan. Cut 4 tortillas into thin (½-inch/12 mm or less) strips. Once the oil has reached about 350°F (175°C), or it bubbles up when you drop a strip in it, fry the tortilla strips. Fry the strips until golden brown, about 1 minute, and transfer to a paper towel–lined plate. Season with salt.

PREP: Separate the leaves of 3 heads lettuce and tear them into bite-size pieces; wash and spin dry. Cut 1 pint (280 g) cherry tomatoes in half. Halve, pit, and peel 1 avocado and cut into eighths. Thinly slice 2 Persian cucumbers and slice some chives.

ASSEMBLE AND SERVE: Arrange the lettuce on a serving platter. Arrange the tomatoes, cucumbers, and avocado on the serving platter. Peel the eggs, cut them into quarters, and arrange on the plate. Crumble ½ pound Snoop-style bacon and sprinkle evenly over the salad. Crumble 2 ounces (55 g) blue cheese and sprinkle it evenly over everything.

Slice the chicken on a diagonal and transfer to the top of the salad. Drizzle with the dressing and sprinkle with the chives, tortilla strips, and black pepper.

STYLING TIP

Cluster the halved tomatoes and cucumbers in one area of the plate but scatter a few for visual appeal to break things up a bit.

charred corn, tomatoes, halloumi, and chili crisp

Salty, spicy, and sweet—you can have it all in just minutes. Halloumi is a firm, briny cheese usually made from goat's or sheep's milk—it sears and gets amazing, charred flavor when grilled, but doesn't melt completely. It makes a really great vegetarian option when grilling, but the truth is, everyone will love it.

PRODUCE

4 ears sweet corn

2 large heirloom tomatoes

1 handful fresh basil

DAIRY

8 ounces (225 g) halloumi cheese, sliced into 4 pieces

PANTRY

Neutral oil, for the grill

Kosher salt and freshly ground black pepper

Chili Crisp (page 260)

PREP: Preheat a grill to medium-high, about 425°F (220°C).

Pull most of the outer husks of 4 ears corn down to expose the kernels so you can remove the silk. Use a paper towel or a vegetable brush to knock off any stubborn stands. Pull the husks back up. Soak in cold water for about 30 minutes before grilling to prevent the husks from burning—make sure to pat dry before placing on the grill.

COOK: Oil the grates of the grill and then place the corn on the grill. Grill until charred on all sides and the corn is tender, about 15 minutes. Remove the corn and let the ears cool just until they are cool enough to handle, then pull the husks down and return them to the grill for a few minutes, so the kernels get a little char on them, about 5 minutes. Remove from the grill and let cool again until you can handle them comfortably.

Slice 8 ounces (225 g) haloumi into 4 pieces and grill until soft and nicely charred, about 3 minutes per side.

PREP THE VEGETABLES: Slowly and carefully but with commitment and confidence, stand the corn cob upright and slice off the kernels; transfer to a bowl. Cut 2 tomatoes into 1-inch (2.5 cm) thick wedges and add to the bowl with the corn. Season with salt and pepper.

ASSEMBLE AND SERVE: Scatter the sliced tomatoes and grilled corn on a serving platter. Cut the charred halloumi in half on the diagonal to create 8 triangles and place on top of the corn and tomatoes. Drizzle a generous amount of chili crisp over the top and sprinkle with 1 handful basil.

esquites (mexican corn salad)

SERVES 4 AS A SIDE

I love wandering the markets and walking down the streets of Mexico City in the intense heat of the midday sun, until I'm dragging my feet and completely dehydrated. But I'm never hungry. The sweet aroma of fresh masa cooking and the sounds of onions sizzling make it impossible to not try almost everything I see. Elote, in particular, I cannot pass up—delicious, sweet corn on the cob smothered in mayonnaise and salty cheese, with the hot sun on your face as you walk home from Roma Norte. The next best thing to having the real thing is making it this way, at home.

PRODUCE

6 ears sweet corn

2 limes

1 handful fresh cilantro leaves

DAIRY

⅓ cup (40 g) grated cotija cheese

PANTRY

Neutral oil, for the grill

⅓ cup (75 ml) mayonnaise

Kosher salt

Ancho chile powder

PREP: Preheat a grill to medium-high—about 425°F (220°C).

Pull most of the outer husks of 6 ears corn down to expose the kernels so you can remove the silk. Use a paper towel or a vegetable brush to knock off any stubborn stands. Pull the husks back up. Soak in cold water for about 30 minutes before grilling to prevent the husks from burning—make sure to pat dry before placing on the grill.

COOK: Oil the grates of the grill and then place the corn on the grill. Grill until charred on all sides and the corn is tender, about 15 minutes. Remove the corn and let the ears cool just until they are cool enough to handle, then pull the husks down and return them to the grill for a few minutes, so the kernels get a little char on them, about 5 minutes. Remove from the grill and let cool again until you can handle them comfortably.

Working confidently, carefully, and taking your time, hold the corn cobs upright and use your knife to cut off the kernels.

MAKE THE CREAMY LIME DRESSING: In a small bowl, combine ⅓ cup (75 ml) mayonnaise and the zest of 1 lime and season with a bit of salt.

ASSEMBLE AND SERVE: Use the back of a spoon to swoop the dressing along the edge of a serving plate or shallow bowl. Scatter the corn on top. Sprinkle with ⅓ cup (40 g) cotija cheese, then with a generous amount of ancho chile powder and cilantro and serve with lime wedges.

raw zucchini, corn, chile, lime, mint, and more lime

SERVES 4 TO 6 AS A SIDE
(GREAT WITH GRILLED CHICKEN, STEAK, OR FISH)

One summer day I rushed back like a maniac from an upstate meditation retreat to have a barbeque. Any calming effect that the three-day retreat had on me, gone, I just wanted to make something as fast as possible. We had this, and lots of tomatoes with a creamy salsa verde, and bread, and all the moodiness just melted away. Next time, instead of spending too much money on a weekend at Omega, maybe I'll just swing by the farmers' market and remember the transformative powers of corn and butter in the middle of the summer.

PRODUCE

4 to 6 ears sweet corn

2 cloves garlic, thinly sliced

3 limes

1 large zucchini (about ½ pound/225 g)

1 cup (30 g) fresh basil leaves

PANTRY

2 tablespoons extra-virgin olive oil

2 tablespoons unsalted butter

½ teaspoon crushed Calabrian chiles (or crushed red pepper flakes)

Kosher salt and freshly ground black pepper

PREP: Remove the husks from 4 to 6 ears sweet corn. Carefully hold each cob upright and slice the kernels off the cob. Sometimes I like to do this over a rimmed baking sheet because it kind of goes everywhere, but it's really not so bad if you do it slowly and carefully.

COOK: Heat a large cast-iron skillet over medium-high heat. Add 2 tablespoons oil, and once it's shimmering add the corn and 2 cloves sliced garlic. Cook, stirring occasionally, until the corn is deep golden brown in spots, about 4 minutes. Add 2 tablespoons butter and ½ teaspoon crushed chiles and cook for 1 minute. Zest and juice 1 lime into the pan. Transfer from the pan to a plate and let cool a bit.

ASSEMBLE AND SERVE: Trim one end off of 1 large zucchini on a sharp diagonal. Shave the zucchini quite thinly on a mandoline, about the thickness of two coins stacked together. Arrange the zucchini on a serving plate and sprinkle the warm corn on top. Scatter 1 cup (30 g) basil leaves on top, season with salt and pepper, and serve with 2 limes cut into wedges to squeeze on top.

grilled paillards with corn, peaches, and pickled onion

SERVES 2 TO 4 AS A MEAL

I love to make paillards when I'm entertaining because they are easy to eat, and you don't have to stand over the grill for too long. They're also delicious at room temperature, so they can be made in advance to be ready to eat when guests arrive. Making a flavorful salad to put on top of a chicken breast guarantees every bite will be delicious—and this one is filled with some of the best flavors of peak summer. Double it, triple it—this recipe is super simple to adapt to feed any crowd, large or small.

PRODUCE

1 small red onion

2 cloves garlic

2 ears sweet corn

2 peaches

½ cup (15 g) fresh basil leaves

MEAT

2 boneless, skinless chicken breasts, pounded thin or butterflied

PANTRY

½ cup (120 ml) red wine vinegar

A touch of honey

Kosher salt and freshly ground black pepper

Extra-virgin olive oil

Neutral oil, for the grill

2 tablespoons Lacto-Fermented Fresno Chiles (page 256)

PREP: Thinly slice 1 red onion. In a small bowl, combine the onion, ½ cup (120 ml) red wine vinegar, a touch of honey, and a bit of salt. Let sit for up to a day while you finish prepping, tossing around once in a while.

Peel 2 cloves garlic by smashing them with the side of the knife. Chop as finely as you can, and then sprinkle 2 teaspoons salt over the garlic. Using the side of your knife, smooth it into a paste. Rub this paste all over 2 pounded chicken breasts and rub with a good amount of olive oil. Let sit for about 30 minutes or so at room temperature, or put in an airtight container and let sit in the fridge for up to a day.

Pull most of the outer husks of 2 ears corn down to expose the kernels so you can remove the silk. Use a paper towel or a vegetable brush to knock off any stubborn strands. Pull the husks back up. Soak in cold water for about 30 minutes before grilling to prevent the husks from burning—make sure to pat dry before placing on the grill.

COOK: Preheat a grill to medium-high (375 to 450°F/195 to 230°C).

Oil the grates of the grill and then place the corn on the grill. Grill until charred on all sides and the corn is tender, about 15 minutes. Remove the corn and let the ears cool just until they are cool enough to handle, then pull the husks down and return them to the grill for a few minutes, so the kernels get a little char on them, about 5 minutes. Remove from the grill and let cool again until you can handle them comfortably.

Place the chicken on the grill and cook, turning, until charred on both sides and cooked through—about 10 minutes total.

ASSEMBLE AND SERVE: Put the chicken on plates or a platter. Carefully cut the kernels off of the cobs and into a medium bowl. Thinly slice 2 peaches and put them in the bowl, along with 2 tablespoons pickled chiles and ½ cup (65 g) pickled onion plus 2 tablespoons of the juice. Season with salt and pepper. Add ½ cup (15 g) basil just before serving. Put the salad on top of the chicken.

grilled nectarines with gorgonzola, honey, and hazelnuts

SERVES 4 AS AN AFTER-DINNER TREAT

As the summer progresses, nectarines will continue to sweeten—and you'll be able to find freestone varieties at the market (stone fruit that easily separates from its pit). That's the best kind for this recipe—grilling them in halves just makes them easier to handle. Grilling fruits also enhances their natural sweetness, and serving them slightly warm with a drizzle of local honey and slightly tangy gorgonzola makes for an almost effortless dessert that is just right for finishing a summer meal.

COOK: Preheat a grill to medium-high heat (375 to 450°F/195 to 230°C). Cut 4 nectarines in half and remove the pits. Drizzle with a bit of oil and grill until charred and warmed through, about 3 minutes per side.

ASSEMBLE AND SERVE: Transfer the nectarines to a serving platter, drizzle with 3 tablespoons honey, and sprinkle with ½ cup (70 g) crumbled gorgonzola and ½ cup (15 g) mint leaves. Roughly chop ½ cup (70 g) toasted hazelnuts and sprinkle them over the platter, along with a bit of flaky salt.

PRODUCE
4 ripe but not too ripe freestone nectarines or peaches

½ cup (15 g) fresh mint leaves

DAIRY
½ cup (70 g) crumbled gorgonzola cheese

PANTRY
Extra-virgin olive oil

3 tablespoons honey

½ cup (70 g) hazelnuts, toasted (see page 20)

Flaky salt

peach, cucumber, avocado, dukkah

(TRY IT WITH CHICKEN OR GRILLED SWORDFISH OR SHRIMP.) SERVES 4 AS A SIDE

Sometimes when it's hot enough outside, you're hungry but you just don't know what you could possibly make to eat, and nothing besides tomatoes are really appealing but you've already had tomatoes for breakfast and lunch—this salad is a good solution. Light but substantial, it comes together in minutes. Have it for breakfast with a bit of plain yogurt, or alongside a piece of swordfish or some grilled chicken or shrimp, or just by itself with an ice-cold glass of wine.

PREP: Thinly slice 2 peaches and put in a large bowl. Halve, pit, and peel 1 avocado, thinly slice, and add to the bowl. Slice 2 Persian cucumbers into ¼-inch (6 mm) rounds and add to the bowl, along with ½ cup (210 g) ciliegine mozzarella, and toss to combine.

ASSEMBLE AND SERVE: Transfer to a platter. Drizzle with oil and sprinkle with plenty of dukkah and flaky salt. Squeeze 1 lime over everything.

PRODUCE
2 ripe peaches
1 avocado
2 Persian cucumbers
1 lime

DAIRY
½ cup (210 g) fresh ciliegine mozzarella

PANTRY
Extra-virgin olive oil (use your good stuff)
Dukkah (page 261)
Flaky salt

168

smashed cucumbers

(IT'S AN IDEAL PART OF YOUR FAVORITE RICE BOWL.)

SERVES 2 TO 4 AS A STARTER OR SIDE

Once I spent the day working with Madhur Jaffrey in her incredible church-turned-studio somewhere near the Berkshires. I was just assisting, so I didn't get to say a word to her all day, and then, as I was packing up—she leaned over and said, "Leave any leftover cucumbers for me. I'm a total cucumber freak." I'm a cucumber freak too. Especially in the summer months, I'll just walk around eating them whole. These crushed cucumbers make a perfect light meal over a bowl of rice—sometimes I make myself a little tuna with Kewpie mayonnaise and sriracha or sprinkle with a bit of bonito flakes to make a sushi-inspired dinner in minutes.

PREP: Using the side of a chef's knife or cleaver, use the palm of your hand to smack the blade down on each of 4 Japanese or 8 Persian cucumbers, smashing it. Once it's split up a bit, chop into bite-size pieces, place in a colander, and sprinkle with a good amount of salt. Let sit for about 5 minutes. Transfer to a bowl and sprinkle with rice vinegar and toss—you want enough vinegar in there that the cucumbers can soak a bit and lightly pickle. Let them sit for another 10 minutes or up to a few hours, tossing once in a while to make sure everything gets coated.

ASSEMBLE AND SERVE: Drain the cucumbers, drizzle with a bit of hot sesame oil, and sprinkle with toasted sesame seeds and bonito flakes, if using.

PRODUCE

4 Japanese or English cucumbers, or 8 Persian cucumbers

PANTRY

Kosher salt

Unseasoned rice vinegar

Hot sesame oil

Toasted sesame seeds

Bonito flakes (optional)

cucumber breakfast salad

SERVES 2 AS BREAKFAST

This recipe is for Thomas Joseph, director of all things food at Martha Stewart, friend, cucumber freak, Virgo, and one of the most talented men I know. We have made so many salads together, and so many strange snacks—some great, like this one, others too foul to mention (lettuce and tomato sauce should never be mixed). He has taught me many important lessons throughout the years, but perhaps "Don't be stingy" is one of the best. Use plenty of seeds on this—they give great flavor and crunch—and use your best olive oil, as it makes a big difference. It's also great served with a slice of sourdough or pita.

COOK: Heat a small sauté pan over medium heat. Add 1 tablespoon coriander seeds and 1 teaspoon cumin seeds and toast, swirling the pan around a bit, until fragrant and golden, about 4 minutes. Transfer the seeds to a mortar and pestle (or to a cutting board to whack with something heavy or chop with a serrated knife) and crush the seeds a bit.

ASSEMBLE AND SERVE: Divide ½ cup (120 ml) yogurt between two bowls and swirl nicely with the back of the spoon to create a swoop. Slice 2 Persian cucumbers into ¼-inch (6 mm) rounds and scatter them on top of the yogurt. Halve and pit 1 avocado, and scoop it out of its skin, and thinly slice, arranging half an avocado in each bowl. Peel and halve 2 cooked eggs and snuggle them into the bowls. Drizzle with a generous amount of your luxe olive oil and sprinkle with flaky salt, 1 handful cilantro, and cilantro blossoms, if you have them, and serve with a few lemon wedges on the side.

PRODUCE

2 Persian cucumbers

1 avocado

1 handful fresh cilantro leaves (and some blossoms if you can find them)

1 lemon

DAIRY

½ cup (120 ml) plain Greek-style yogurt

2 jammy or hard-boiled eggs (see page 263)

PANTRY

1 tablespoon whole coriander seeds

1 teaspoon cumin seeds

Extra-virgin olive oil

Flaky salt

cucumber and labneh with fruit and rose za'atar

Kismet in Los Angeles has a wonderful cucumber salad that changes often depending on what fruit is in season. I love all of the unexpected flavors I've had there—persimmon in the winter, cherries in the late spring, melon in the summer—but here I use goldenberries, because that's what was available at my market that day. I do suggest mixing it up with whatever looks appealing at the market; you can't really go wrong. If you don't feel like making your own za'atar, or are put off by rose, instead of using store-bought za'atar I suggest using a bit of sumac, toasted sesame seeds, and fresh mint—it will taste so much fresher.

PREP: In a small bowl, stir together ¼ cup (60 ml) labneh, the zest of 1 blood orange, and 1 tablespoon orange juice. Season with kosher salt.

Cut 1 cup (145 g) goldenberries in half (or thinly slice 2 persimmons, supreme 1 orange, or cut about 1 cup/190 g cantaloupe). Thinly slice 2 cucumbers.

ASSEMBLE AND SERVE: Put a scoop of labneh on each plate, and using the back of your spoon, drag it across the plate and make a swoosh that arches about halfway around the plate. Scatter the goldenberries and cucumbers on the plate. Drizzle with a bit of olive oil and 1 tablespoon orange juice. Sprinkle with a bit of za'atar and flaky sea salt.

PRODUCE

1 blood orange

1 cup (145 g) goldenberries, 2 Fuyu persimmons, 1 orange, or 1 cup (190 g) cantaloupe

2 Persian cucumbers

DAIRY

¼ cup (60 ml) labneh or thick Greek-style yogurt

PANTRY

Kosher salt

Drizzle of extra-virgin olive oil

Sprinkle of Rose Petal Za'atar (page 262)

Flaky sea salt

STYLING TIP

The swoosh seems like a cheffy technique, but it's an easy way to elevate plating at home (plus it makes sure you get plenty of whatever you're schmearing on every bite). You can use a special plating spoon with an offset handle (see page 23), but any spoon will do. Start with a good-size blob, and using the back of your spoon flick your wrist to create a crescent shape on the plate. For platters, just go ahead and coat the whole bottom.

I loved him before he broke the melon open with his hands, but that day on the beach was one of my favorite days and stands out in my memory—one of those that makes me laugh when I'm angry and believe in my bones that it's right. I get sort of drunk off of the summer anyway with the heat and sun and the ripe fruits and long days. It was a sticky mess in his chest hair and on the sandy towel, but the cantaloupe was so sweet and almost musky and, of course, just out of the cooler and ice cold.

There is nothing in the summer like fruit on ice. A tower of melon balls, a big wide bowl of bright red cherries, sweet strawberries, apricots, plums—put it all on ice. Put your vegetables on ice too. It's elegant, yes, but it's just so enjoyable to eat. Refreshing—remember out on the terrace when it had to be 100 degrees? It makes me salivate thinking about it.

It's not exclusive to the summer, but that's when it's best. Or anywhere that makes your skin hot to the touch and every drop of your energy is pulled out of your body by the sun and the salt water.

Every Valentine's Day I love to make a platter of bright red fruits. Pomegranates, tart currants, slippery supremes of blood orange flesh. I would pay ten times as much for anything served on a bed of crushed ice— and I have. In Tokyo we had crudités in an oversized martini glass filled with ice and I think there were maybe six little bites in there to dip in the aioli, but I was in absolute heaven.

This is a love note to fruit on ice, and it's a love note to you too, Ben.

balled melon as a snack

I like to lay out on the beach without going near the water until my skin feels like it's actually melting off. I like to feel the sun penetrating down to my bones, to get sweaty, eyelids closing. I like my speech to slow, my limbs to get heavy. I watch my skin deepen shades in a single day, I read a few pages of a book and then need to take a nap.

Sometimes I think I could leave it all behind and go burn out on an island somewhere and just eat fruit. Usually by the time I'm having that thought I remember the bag of melon balls in my cooler.

Like jumping into the cold waves, the feeling of eating an ice-cold melon ball instantly revitalizes and quenches. I don't think there is anything that even comes close. Melons are in peak season in the height of summer and early fall—ripe cantaloupe and honeydew should have a strong sweet scent when held up to your nose, and watermelons should have a nice hollow sound when tapped. You could squeeze some lime juice on the melon balls or chop up a little mint—but I prefer them plain and ice cold.

PRODUCE

1 cantaloupe, halved, seeds scooped

1 honeydew, halved, seeds scooped

1 small seedless watermelon, halved

PREP AND SERVE: Use a melon baller (or a tablespoon measure, or a spring-loaded ice cream scoop) and scoop the flesh of 3 melons into balls—you can tap the baller against the side of the bowl to get the fruit to release. Chill in the fridge for at least an hour, or better yet, serve right on top of a bed of crushed ice.

cantaloupe, cucumbers, lime, and mint

One summer day out in the Rockaways, Lauryn read an article about melons from a 1992 issue of *Saveur* magazine out loud in an Australian accent. It was one of the most relaxing days of all time. Just say it in your head right now. *Meah-lin*.

PRODUCE

1 small, exceptionally ripe cantaloupe

2 Persian or other small cucumbers, or 1 large English cucumber

1 cup fresh mint leaves

2 limes

PANTRY

Large pinch of your favorite chili powder, such as Tajín seasoning

Flaky salt

PREP: Cut the ends of 1 cantaloupe so it has two flat surfaces. While it's on one of its flat surfaces, cut the rind off the melon, trying to lose as little flesh as possible. Cut the melon in half, scoop out the seeds. Cut in half again, and thinly slice.

ASSEMBLE AND SERVE: Shingle the melon on a platter (on top of ice if you can; if not, chill just the melon and cucumber on the platter, covered in the fridge, for an hour or so before serving). Thinly slice 2 cucumbers on an extreme diagonal and snuggle the slices into the melon. Scatter 1 cup mint leaves on top. Squeeze a little lime juice over it, and cut the rest of the limes into wedges for serving. Sprinkle with a generous amount of chili powder (depending how spicy you like it) and a good amount of flaky salt.

honeydew, feta, jalapeños, and lime

SERVES 6 TO 8 AS A SNACK

If you took out the feta cheese, I'm certain that if blended, this would also make an incredible tequila-based cocktail.

PRODUCE

1 small, extremely ripe honeydew melon

1 small jalapeño or serrano chile

2 limes

1 cup fresh basil leaves (torn, if large; I recommend purple basil, if available)

DAIRY

4 ounces (115 g) feta cheese (Valbreso or French)

PANTRY

Extra-virgin olive oil (the good stuff)

Flaky salt

PREP: Cut the ends of 1 honeydew melon so it has two flat surfaces. While it's on one of its flat surfaces, cut the rind off the melon, trying to lose as little flesh as possible. Cut the melon in half and scoop out the seeds. Cut in half again and thinly slice.

ASSEMBLE AND SERVE: Shingle the melon slices on a platter. Thinly slice 4 ounces (115 g) feta and add the thin shards to the platter with the melon. Thinly slice 1 jalapeño (I like to do it on a mandoline, and I keep the seeds in for a little extra kick) and scatter it on top of the melon and feta. Use a Microplane to zest 1 lime right over the platter, then squeeze its juice all over. Cut another lime into wedges and arrange around the platter. Drizzle the salad with oil and sprinkle with flaky salt. Add 1 cup basil to the platter.

watermelon, shiso, plum, and salt

One hot summer evening, my friend Jason and I decided to stay in the AC and watch Werner Herzog's documentary about the internet. I had gone to the Japanese grocery store earlier that day and had bought ume shiso salt (a salty, tangy, sour-tart MSG sprinkle made from shiso and plum), and he brought over a whole watermelon. The combination of those two things are simply divine, and we ate the entire melon before the film was over. But if you use fresh plums and shiso, you'll take the experience up another notch. You can usually find fresh shiso at your local farmers' market or Japanese market. It's not quite basil-y; it's citrusy, perfumey, and a little bit . . . savory? The purple variety gives umeboshi (Japanese pickled plum) it's beautiful pink color, but any variety of shiso will work for this. For a little kick, a bit of togarashi (an incredible Japanese spice mixture) is very special.

PRODUCE

1 small seedless watermelon (about 4 pounds)

3 black plums (or a green one if you can find it!)

10 fresh shiso leaves

PANTRY

Lots of flaky salt

Sprinkle of togarashi (optional)

PREP: Cut the watermelon in half and scoop out the seeds. Cut in half again, and thinly slice.

ASSEMBLE AND SERVE: Shingle the watermelon on a platter. Thinly slice the plums and snuggle them into the watermelon.

Roll 5 shiso leaves up like a little cigar and run the blade of your very sharp knife over them to slice them extremely thinly. Do this with the remaining 5 leaves. Sprinkle your chiffonade over the watermelon and plums. Sprinkle with a generous amount of flaky salt and a little togarashi, if using.

dilly double beans and farro

It was the height of summer, probably an August evening. I went over to my friend David's photo studio and he had made me the absolute perfect summer meal—a bright lemony farro and green bean salad (the beans still green and crisp with handfuls and handfuls of dill), a simple, fresh sweet corn and cherry tomato salad, and roasted chicken. I suggest that you replicate that entire meal if you can, making sure to move your table so it's right by an open window, then add plenty of candles, delicious wine, and the very best company you can find.

PRODUCE

1 pound (455 g) green beans

3 cloves garlic, peeled

2 lemons

½ cup (25 g) chopped fresh dill

PANTRY

1 cup (200 g) farro

Kosher salt and freshly ground black pepper

2 tablespoons toasted walnut oil, or extra-virgin olive oil

¼ to ½ teaspoon crushed red pepper flakes

1 (15-ounce/430 g) can cannellini beans

½ cup (50 g) walnuts, toasted (see page 20)

COOK: Fill a medium pot with cold water. Add 1 cup (200 g) farro and double check the package instructions, because there are a few different kinds of farro out there and I don't want to lead you astray. Cook until the farro is tender but a bit of tooth remains.

Set up an ice bath. Fill a pot of water and bring it to a boil. This time, salt it heavily. Trim 1 pound (455 g) green beans, cut them in half, and add to the boiling water. Cook just to take the raw off them, until they are bright green, about 2 minutes. Drain and transfer to the ice bath. Once completely cool, transfer to paper towels or a clean kitchen towel.

MAKE THE LEMON WALNUT DILL VINAIGRETTE: Grate 3 cloves garlic into a large bowl using a Microplane. Zest 2 lemons into the bowl, and juice ½ of one those lemons (about 2 tablespoons juice) right into the bowl. Whisk in 2 tablespoons toasted walnut oil, ¼ to ½ teaspoon red pepper flakes, and ½ cup (25 g) chopped dill. Season with salt and pepper.

ASSEMBLE AND SERVE: Drain and rinse 1 (15-ounce/430 g) can cannellini beans and add them, along with the cooked farro, to the bowl with the dressing, then toss to combine. Check seasoning and add salt and pepper to taste. If serving later at room temperature, which is a great way to enjoy this salad, wait to top with the toasted walnuts so they don't get soggy. Transfer to a serving bowl or plates and cut the remaining zested lemon into wedges to serve on the side.

crunchy beans

I've never really understood the appeal of three-bean salad, but it mysteriously appears at every barbecue I've ever been to. I don't like anything to be mushy, so I've made everything crunchy and bright in this bean salad, and it feels really fresh and like something I may have more than one helping of.

PRODUCE

1 bunch radishes

½ small white onion

1 English or regular cucumber

¾ pound (340 g) haricots verts

PANTRY

Kosher salt

1 recipe Lemony Yogurt Vinaigrette (page 259)

1 recipe Crispy Chickpeas (page 260)

Ground sumac

PREP: Make an ice bath and set a medium pot of salted water on the stove to boil.

Shave the radishes with a mandoline directly into the ice bath. Shave ½ white onion with the mandoline directly into the ice bath. Let them crisp up for about 10 minutes. Thinly slice 1 cucumber on a diagonal. Snip the tops from ¾ pound (340 g) haricots verts.

COOK: Add the haricot verts to the boiling water and just cook the raw off, about 2 minutes, and no more! Immediately transfer to the ice bath.

ASSEMBLE AND SERVE: Drain the vegetables and dry everything off really well on a clean kitchen towel or paper towels. Transfer the radishes, onion, cucumber, and haricots verts to a serving platter, tossing them together as you go. Drizzle with the vinaigrette. Top with the crispy chickpeas and a good sprinkle of sumac.

charred broccoli soba bowl with peanut sauce

My dad loves peanut butter so much that when there was a recall because of an E. coli scare, he lasted just a few days before eating it again because he said he just couldn't live without it. I kind of feel the same way. Anything is delicious smothered in peanut butter, but charred broccoli really does it for me. At first glance this recipe seems a little fussy, but after you make it once, you'll be making it all the time. It packs well for lunch. Hold the fish sauce to make it vegan.

PRODUCE

1 head broccoli

1 lime

3 Persian cucumbers, or 1 English cucumber

3 scallions, thinly sliced

1 handful fresh basil leaves

1 handful fresh cilantro leaves

1 handful fresh mint leaves

PANTRY

1 (16-ounce/455 g) package firm or extra-firm tofu

Chili Crisp (page 260), or neutral oil, such as peanut or avocado, and 1 to 2 teaspoons crushed red pepper flakes

Kosher salt

2 bundles (6 ounces/170 g) soba or rice noodles

¼ cup (60 ml) crunchy natural peanut butter

1 tablespoon soy sauce

1 to 2 teaspoons fish sauce (optional)

1 teaspoon honey

3 tablespoons warm water

PREP: Preheat the oven to 425°F (220°C).

Set a few layers of paper towels or clean kitchen towels on a large plate or rimmed baking sheet. Cut 1 (16-ounce/455 g) block of tofu lengthwise into 4 rectangles and set them down on top of towels, and then put another layer of towels on top of the tofu. Put a cast-iron skillet or another plate with something heavy like a can of tomatoes on top and let the tofu get squeezed for about 15 or 20 minutes (you can do this overnight—but don't skip this step; it really improves the tofu's texture).

Cut 1 head broccoli into florets.

COOK: Transfer the tofu and broccoli florets to a rimmed baking sheet. Drizzle with 2 tablespoons of the chili crisp oil (not the crispy part or the flakes—that's for later), or 2 tablespoons neutral oil with 1 to 2 teaspoons red pepper flakes, and sprinkle with salt. Roast until the tofu is golden and the broccoli is charred, about 25 to 30 minutes, flipping once.

Bring a medium pot of water to a boil and cook 2 bundles soba or rice noodles according to the package instructions, then drain and run under cold water until chilled.

MAKE THE PEANUT SAUCE: In a large bowl, whisk together ¼ cup (60 ml) peanut butter, 1 tablespoon soy sauce, 1 to 2 teaspoons fish sauce, if using, 1 teaspoon honey, and the juice of ½ lime and add warm water 1 tablespoon at a time until the desired consistency is reached—you may have to add more or less based on your PB.

ASSEMBLE AND SERVE: Slice 3 Persian or 1 English cucumber in half lengthwise. Cut into ¼-inch (6 mm) slices on a sharp diagonal and add to the bowl with the dressing. Add the noodles to the bowl and toss to combine. Divide the noodle mixture between two shallow serving bowls. Top with the tofu, broccoli, and a generous spoonful of chili crisp. Sprinkle 3 sliced scallions and 1 handful each of basil, cilantro, and mint on top and serve with ½ lime cut into wedges.

grilled broccolini with green goddess and quinoa crunch

SERVES 2 AS A MAIN DISH

One summer my friend Penny rented a house on Little Cranberry Island in Maine. A few of us flew into Bangor, then took a water taxi to picturesque New England summer heaven. Penny picked us up by golf cart, speeding down the dirt paths, past weather-beaten shingled homes. The house was right next to the sea, and we spent our mornings stoned, picking blueberries until we got tired of it. Norah and I cooked at night. Norah is a fantastic cook and food stylist. When food is your thing, it can really mess up your flow cooking with another cook, but we had so much fun just making food for pleasure, riffing off of each other with produce from the farm and fish caught that day. This is one of the many dishes we made. Thank you, Norah, for introducing me to the quinoa crunch.

PRODUCE

3 heads broccolini, ends trimmed

1 lemon

PANTRY

½ cup (85 g) quinoa

Extra-virgin olive oil

Kosher salt and freshly ground black pepper

Neutral oil, for frying

1 recipe Green Goddess Dressing (page 262)

COOK: Put ½ cup (85 g) quinoa in a fine-mesh sieve and run it under cold water to rinse for a minute. Add 1 scant cup (200 ml) water to a small pot and bring to a boil. Add the quinoa, bring back to a simmer, cover, and cook for 17 minutes. Keep the lid on and let it steam for about 5 minutes. Fluff up with a fork, and then transfer to a rimmed baking sheet. Let cool and dry off (this will take about 30 minutes—really make sure it's dry!).

Meanwhile, get your grill or grill pan heating over high heat. Trim the ends from 3 heads broccolini and toss in a couple of tablespoons olive oil and season with salt and pepper. Add the broccolini to the grill and cook until well charred and crisp-tender, about 4 minutes per side.

Heat about ¼ inch (6 mm) neutral oil in a 10-inch (25 cm) nonstick skillet. Set up a fine-mesh sieve over a heatproof bowl. Drop a piece of quinoa into the oil, and if it bubbles up like crazy, the oil is ready to go. Working in batches if necessary, carefully add some of the quinoa and push it around with a wooden spoon. Cook until golden brown, 4 to 5 minutes. Drain in the sieve, then transfer to a paper towel–lined rimmed baking sheet or plate. Season with salt.

ASSEMBLE AND SERVE: Smear 1 recipe green goddess dressing on a serving platter. Scatter the grilled broccolini on top, then sprinkle with the quinoa crisp. Serve with lemon wedges on the side.

192

zucchini ribbons with pecorino, mint, and almonds

SERVES 4 TO 6 AS A SIDE (I LOVE THIS SERVED OVER GRILLED CHICKEN PAILLARDS OR A FIRM FISH WITH LOTS OF LEMON.)

I remember making this salad for lunch for Martha when I was an intern. She ate it in the kitchen; it was just the two of us. Everyone was nervous. They warned me that she wouldn't like the raw zucchini, that she didn't like wet things. She didn't say a thing about the zucchini, but did tell me she liked it, even though she doesn't usually like both nuts and cheese in her salads. This salad is so simple, that's why I think it passed the test.

PRODUCE
1 lemon

2 zucchini

½ cup (15 g) fresh mint leaves

DAIRY
Pecorino cheese

PANTRY
Extra-virgin olive oil

2 teaspoons Champagne vinegar

Kosher salt and freshly ground black pepper

½ cup (70 g) whole almonds, toasted (see page 20) and chopped

MAKE THE LEMONY CHAMPAGNE VINAIGRETTE (WITHOUT MUSTARD): In a large bowl, combine about 2 tablespoons oil, 2 teaspoons Champagne vinegar, the zest of 1 lemon, and the juice of ½ lemon. Season with salt and pepper.

PREP: Peel 2 zucchini into long, thin ribbons with a mandoline or Y-peeler.

ASSEMBLE AND SERVE: Toss the zucchini ribbons, ½ cup (70 g) almonds (chopped), and ½ cup (15 g) mint in the dressing. Using your Y-peeler, peel strips of cheese right over the salad, or if you prefer, make a mountain of fluffy shredded cheese using a Microplane. Season with salt and pepper.

STYLING TIP

Make sure some of the zucchini ribbons are folded a bit when you are piling them on the plate, creating some volume so they are not all lying flat.

lemony chicken salad

MAKES ABOUT 4 CUPS/700 G (SERVE AS SANDWICHES OR LETTUCE CUPS, OR JUST DIP CRACKERS IN IT AS A SNACK.)

I love chicken salad, and it's a perfect example of why sometimes simpler is just better. Sure, you could add yogurt, or avocado, or lots of herbs—or even grapes or nuts—but I think the brightness of lemon zest and a little parsley are all you need. My favorite way to eat it is with crackers at the beach or as an open-faced sandwich with lettuce.

PRODUCE

1 cup (50 g) chopped fresh parsley

2 lemons

Crispy lettuce, for serving

MEAT

3 to 4 cups (585 to 780 g) chicken meat pulled from 1 cooked chicken (rotisserie is fine)

PANTRY

¼ cup plus 2 tablespoons (90 ml) mayonnaise (you may have to add another tablespoon or two if your chicken is larger!)

Kosher salt and freshly ground black pepper

Crispy lettuce (such as Little Gem or Butterhead) and toast or crackers, for serving

ASSEMBLE AND SERVE: Chop up 3 to 4 cups (585 to 780 g) chicken meat a bit—depending on how chunky you like it. In a large bowl, combine the chicken, ¼ cup plus 2 tablespoons (90 ml) mayonnaise, 1 cup (50 g) chopped parsley, and the zest of 2 lemons. Season with salt and pepper. Serve with crispy lettuce, such as Little Gem or Butterhead, lemon wedges, and toast; or with crackers.

shrimp louie salad

SERVES 2 TO 4 AS A MEAL

The first time I had a Shrimp Louie salad I was in Ventura, California, while traveling on a Food & Wine tour with Martha. I don't remember when it was exactly, but it was still very cold back in New York. I had the day off, and with short sleeves on and the sun shining I walked to the boardwalk in the afternoon for lunch. I had the Shrimp Louie, with canned black olives and iceberg lettuce, and it was perfect—it was everything I wanted and thought I should be eating on a Southern California afternoon. I loved it so much that I went back again for dinner and ruined some of the magic. I got greedy and there is such a thing as too much shrimp. This is the perfect summer lunch salad. I've made it for ladies playing bridge in the Hamptons. I imagine someday I'll make it after playing tennis. It's best enjoyed with a white wine spritzer over lots of ice or a Diet Coke with lemon. It is, to me, a certain romanticized California served on a plate—that is to say, a feeling.

PRODUCE
3 lemons

2 heads Little Gem lettuce

1 cup (145 g) cherry tomatoes

1 avocado

2 Persian cucumbers

Fresh dill

DAIRY
2 large eggs

MEAT
1 pound (455 g) shrimp (16 to 20), shell on, fresh or frozen

PANTRY
2 bay leaves

1 teaspoon black peppercorns

¼ cup (60 ml) mayonnaise

1 teaspoon tomato paste

1 teaspoon white vinegar

1 teaspoon Tabasco sauce

Kosher salt and freshly ground black pepper

COOK: Prepare an ice bath. Fill a medium pot with water to 2 to 3 inches (5 to 7.5 cm) below the rim and add 2 halved lemons, 2 bay leaves, and 1 teaspoon black peppercorns. Bring to a boil, then reduce to a gentle simmer. Add 1 pound (455 g) shrimp and cook until bright pink and cooked all the way through—6 minutes for fresh, and about 9 minutes right from frozen.

Transfer the shrimp to the ice bath and empty out the pot, then refill it with fresh water and return to a boil. Add the eggs. Cook for 10 minutes, then transfer to the ice bath.

PREP: Separate the leaves of 2 heads lettuce and tear them into bite-size pieces; wash and spin dry.

ASSEMBLE: Arrange the lettuce on serving plates or a large platter. Cut 1 cup (145 g) cherry tomatoes in half. Cluster the tomatoes in one area of each plate, and scatter a few about the plate. Cut 1 avocado in half and remove the pit. Use a spoon to peel off the skin and cut each half into four wedges. Arrange on the plates. Slice 2 Persian cucumbers on the bias, and cluster in one section of each plate.

Peel the shrimp but leave their tails intact. Arrange the shrimp on the plates. Peel the eggs and cut into quarters. Arrange them on the plates. Pick some small pieces of dill to scatter around the plate, along with plenty of fresh pepper—and lots of lemon wedges.

MAKE THE LOUIE SAUCE AND SERVE: In a small bowl, combine ¼ cup (60 ml) mayonnaise, 1 teaspoon tomato paste, 1 teaspoon white vinegar, and 1 teaspoon Tabasco sauce, and season with salt and pepper. Transfer to a pretty little bowl for serving alongside the salad.

nashville hot chicken salad

The truth is I've only been to Nashville once and it was to see Morrissey perform, and I stopped eating meat for a long time after that, so I have no authority to write an authentic Nashville hot chicken recipe. Really, Ben just loves it so much, and the line at Howlin' Ray's in Los Angeles is too long to wait in, so I had to learn how to make it at home. This recipe is what they might consider "medium" spicy at an authentic spot, but I consider it to be very spicy. Adjust the amount of cayenne if you don't love heat.

PRODUCE

½ head red cabbage

2 stalks celery, plus all the leaves from the whole head of celery

1 bunch scallions

DAIRY

1 cup (240 ml) buttermilk

2 large eggs

1 recipe Garlicky Buttermilk Ranch Dressing (page 259)

MEAT

4 boneless, skinless chicken breasts

PANTRY

Kosher salt and freshly ground black pepper

Neutral oil, for frying

2 cups (255 g) all-purpose flour

1 tablespoon vinegar-based hot sauce, such as Tabasco

3 tablespoons cayenne pepper

1 tablespoon brown sugar

1 teaspoon ancho chile powder

1 teaspoon garlic powder

2 teaspoons hot paprika

½ cup (75 g) sliced pickles (bread and butter or kosher dill)

PREP: Season 4 chicken breasts with 1 tablespoon salt and a generous amount of pepper and place in a zip-top bag for a couple of hours in the fridge. Bring it out about half an hour before you want to fry.

Using a mandoline, thinly slice ½ head cabbage and 2 stalks celery into a large bowl. Thinly slice 1 bunch scallions and add to the bowl, along with all of the celery leaves from the head of celery.

COOK: Preheat about 2 inches (5 cm) oil in a cast-iron Dutch oven or something similar. You'll want to use a candy or deep-frying thermometer to keep the oil temperature at a consistent 325°F (165°C).

In one shallow bowl (or a pie plate), whisk together 1 cup (240 ml) buttermilk and 2 eggs. In another bowl, combine 2 cups (255 g) flour and a good pinch of salt. Dredge the chicken breasts in flour one at a time, then plunge them into the buttermilk bath, allowing the excess to drip off. Dredge the chicken in the flour again. Place on a rimmed baking sheet with a rack inside. Once all are coated you are ready to fry.

Carefully lower the chicken into the pot of oil—you will have to work in at least two batches. You will be looking for a deeply golden exterior on both sides of the chicken, and you'll want the internal temperature to be 165°F (74°C). This should take about 15 minutes, depending on the thickness of your chicken breasts. Set the chicken on a wire cooling rack over a paper bag or paper towels.

Allow the oil in the pot to cool slightly, then scoop about 1 cup (240 ml) of it out very carefully. Transfer it to a heatproof bowl and whisk in 3 tablespoons cayenne, 1 tablespoon brown sugar, 1 teaspoon ancho chile powder, 1 teaspoon garlic powder, and 2 teaspoons hot paprika. Use a brush to paint this hot oil onto your chicken.

ASSEMBLE AND SERVE: Add half of the ranch dressing to the large bowl of cabbage. Add ½ cup (75 g) of whatever pickles you're using and toss to combine. Transfer to a serving platter or plates.

Thinly slice the chicken breast and place on top of the salad. Drizzle with the remaining ranch dressing or serve on the side.

beets, tomatoes, and cilantro

SERVES 4 AS A MEAL

Sarah Carey (the food director at Martha Stewart, formerly my boss, always my second mom) introduced me to this flavor combination. I think she's single-handedly proved to me that adding cilantro to any combination of vegetables is not only delicious, but feels fresh and revelatory every time it's done. This recipe is a perfect way to savor that sweet spot at the end of summer and the beginning of fall when the nights start to get cooler and the last of the juicy tomatoes are plentiful at the market. Get greedy. Buy more than you think you need, or scramble to save the ones left in your garden before the first frost. Serve this with a simple steak or roasted chicken, or eat it alone until there are no more tomatoes left to eat.

PRODUCE

2 bunches red or yellow beets (about 9 medium)

3 to 4 large heirloom tomatoes

1 pint (280 g) cherry tomatoes

½ cup (15 g) fresh cilantro leaves

PANTRY

Extra-virgin olive oil (this is a great time to use your fancy oil)

Kosher salt and freshly ground black pepper

Flaky salt

COOK: Preheat the oven to 425°F (220°C).

Roast 2 bunches trimmed beets in packets with oil and kosher salt and pepper following the instructions on page 263.

PREP: I recommend using a plastic cutting board that can be easily washed for this part. Also, if you have a pair of latex gloves handy, you could wear them to keep your hands from getting stained. If you have different-colored beets, you'll want to keep them separate. Using a paper towel, rub the skins gently to remove them—they should come off quite easily. Clean up your mess and then thinly slice 2 bunches red or yellow beets.

Thinly slice 3 to 4 large heirloom tomatoes and slice 1 pint (280 g) cherry tomatoes in half.

ASSEMBLE AND SERVE: Arrange the beets and tomatoes on plates or a platter. Drizzle with oil. Sprinkle with the cilantro leaves and a little black pepper and flaky salt.

STYLING TIP

This is a great time to showcase a variety of tomatoes. Different colors, shapes, and sizes transform this dish into something really striking and completely irresistible—the more the merrier.

newell's beets

A three-hour drive from New York City will bring you over bright green mountains to a lush little valley called Bovina, where there's not much of a main street besides the one restaurant and a café that serves excellent sandwiches and pie. Have you ever felt so calmed by a place that it felt like home from the first visit?

I spent a summer in Bovina, and it almost feels like it was a dream. Not only is it an incredibly beautiful place, but it's filled with some of the most wonderful, interesting, and talented people I've ever met. One of those people is my friend Newell, a fabulous designer, gardener, and cook. He made the perfect late summer meal that we ate at a big round table covered with a floral cloth in his beautifully manicured flower garden. As a cool breeze crept up through the mountains and the sun set, we started our meal with a beet tartare inspired from a local restaurant called Peekamoose—this is my nod to that salad, that meal, and a wonderful friend.

COOK: Preheat the oven to 425°F (220°C).

Roast 4 bunches trimmed beets in packets with oil, kosher salt and pepper, and the zest of 1 orange, following the instructions on page 263.

MAKE THE TRUFFLED BALSAMIC VINAIGRETTE: In a small bowl, combine 1 teaspoon mustard, 2 tablespoons balsamic vinegar, ½ teaspoon honey, 1 tablespoon mayonnaise, and ⅓ teaspoon truffle oil. Whisk until completely smooth and combined. Season with kosher salt and pepper.

PREP: I recommend using a plastic cutting board that can be easily washed for this part. Also, if you have a pair of latex gloves handy, you could wear them to keep your hands from getting stained. If you have different-colored beets, you'll want to keep them separate. Using a paper towel, rub the skins gently to remove them—they should come off quite easily. Clean up your mess and then thinly slice, or cut into halves, the beets.

ASSEMBLE AND SERVE: Drizzle the dressing on a serving plate or platter. Arrange the sliced beets on top of the vinaigrette and drizzle a bit more on top. Slice the larger caper berries in half and scatter a few smaller ones around the plate. Sprinkle with a little flaky salt and plenty of pepper to serve.

PRODUCE

4 bunches baby beets, preferably a mix of colors

Zest of 1 orange

PANTRY

Extra-virgin olive oil

Kosher salt and freshly ground black pepper

1 teaspoon Dijon mustard

2 tablespoons balsamic vinegar

½ teaspoon honey

1 tablespoon mayonnaise

⅓ teaspoon truffle oil

4 to 6 caperberries, halved

Flaky salt

STYLING TIP

Coating the bottom of the plate when there is a creamy dressing allows the beauty of the ingredients to shine, and it's easy to get some in every bite when it's a scoop-able salad like this one.

fall

I find the early days of fall to be bittersweet. The days are long, and you always seem to catch the sunset and the evenings are just starting to get cool enough to need a sweater. The water is the warmest it will be all year because it has had months to soak up the hot sun, and the beaches are empty—everyone has returned home. Now that the scent of piss and garbage has been blown away by the wonderful breeze, the city sidewalks feel romantic again on evening walks. Maybe growing up in a tourist town like Shelter Island made the post–Labor Day shift more dramatic, but there was always a sadness in the sudden silence just as much as there was a relief—a return to normalcy, to routine.

Some of summer spills into September, the last tomatoes, sometimes the juiciest of all, keep going as long as they can. There are still weekends at the park and dinners outside. As the leaves begin to turn into my favorite palette of bright saffron, mustard, ochre, sienna, rust, and poppy the ingredients too begin to shift in color to deeper, moodier jewel tones. Sweaters turn into jackets, which turn into coats and scarves and hats and windows close and fireplaces are started and the familiar banging of New York City radiators start their clanging and hissing lullaby every night.

By Halloween we'll wake up to a ground coated in sparkling frost, and tomato plants and tender herbs and cucumber vines will be long blackened and shriveled and dead. The bare trees shake in the wind with their sinister twisted branches and the chill of the air goes right to the bone. Who could imagine eating a cucumber now? A melon? Was that lifetimes ago? Our faces and bodies show no sign of ever having seen the sun. The farmers' market will be all carrots and cabbage for months. The breeze becomes a wind that whips your face as you walk on the West Side. But we'll come back indoors and light candles and make our homes cozy and warm and set tables where the people we love can come even closer. We'll feed them and drink good wine, and listen to music until late into the evening, forgetting there is a whole world going on out there.

plum, endive, and gouda with hazelnuts

SERVES 4 TO 6 AS A STARTER OR SIDE

Fall is not all about apples and pears. Deep purple-fleshed, juicy, tart, and sweet plums can be found well into fall and make the perfect complement to the jewel-toned, bitter leaves of the season.

PRODUCE

2 heads red endive or Treviso, leaves separated

2 black plums, thinly sliced

DAIRY

¼ pound (115 g) aged Gouda cheese

PANTRY

1 tablespoon white balsamic vinegar

2 tablespoons extra-virgin olive oil

1 tablespoon grainy mustard

1 teaspoon maple syrup

Kosher salt and freshly ground black pepper

½ cup (70 g) hazelnuts, toasted (see page 20)

MAKE THE MAPLE VINAIGRETTE: In a large bowl, combine 1 tablespoon vinegar, 2 tablespoons oil, 1 tablespoon grainy mustard. and 1 teaspoon maple syrup. Whisk until combined and season with salt and pepper.

PREP: Separate the leaves of 2 heads endive and tear into bite-size pieces; wash and spin dry. Thinly slice 2 plums.

ASSEMBLE AND SERVE: Add the plums and endive to the dressing and toss to combine. Arrange the endive and plums on plates or a platter, sprinkle ½ cup (70 g) toasted hazelnuts on top, and shave a very generous amount of Gouda with a Y-peeler over everything. Finish with a little fresh pepper.

STYLING TIP

Whenever I can, I try to find monochromatic ingredients to add drama and visual appeal to really simple salads like this one; they elevate the whole table. But if you can't find a purple chicory or red-fleshed plum, this recipe will taste just as good!

roasted grapes, endive, and ricotta salata

SERVES 2 TO 4 AS A STARTER OR LIGHT MEAL (I LIKE TO PILE IT ON TOP OF A CRISPY CHICKEN BREAST.)

I love roasted grapes—they feel rich, decadent, sweet, and familiar, like maybe in a past life I was Roman royalty. Once I served some to one of my favorite authors, Etgar Keret, room temperature right out of a Tupperware container, and still it felt very luxurious and worthy of a special guest. This salad comes together very fast, but feels fancy, and features some of the most beautiful colors of the season.

PRODUCE
1 head Romanesco or cauliflower

1 bunch green or muscat grapes (about 3 cups/450 g), some clusters, but mostly just free grapes

2 heads endive

DAIRY
Ricotta salata

PANTRY
Extra-virgin olive oil

Kosher salt and freshly ground black pepper

2 teaspoons grainy mustard

2 teaspoons apple cider vinegar

½ teaspoon honey

½ cup (70 g) hazelnuts, toasted (see page 20)

COOK: Preheat the oven to 425°F (220°C).

Separate 1 head Romanesco into florets. On a rimmed baking sheet, toss the florets with about 2 tablespoons oil and season with salt and pepper. On a separate rimmed baking sheet, toss 1 bunch grapes (mostly separated from the stems) with more oil and some salt and pepper.

Roast, tossing the Romanesco and grapes once, until the Romanesco is golden in spots and the grapes are blistered, about 25 minutes.

MAKE THE APPLE CIDER VINAIGRETTE: In a large bowl, whisk together 2 teaspoons mustard, 2 teaspoons vinegar, ½ teaspoon honey, and 1 tablespoon oil. Season with salt and pepper.

PREP: Separate the leaves of 2 heads endive and tear into bite-size pieces; wash and spin dry.

ASSEMBLE AND SERVE: Toss the roasted Romanesco, loose grapes, and endive in the dressing, and scatter on plates or a platter. Arrange some of the grape clusters on the plates, sprinkle with ½ cup (70 g) toasted hazelnuts, and use a Y-peeler to shave a generous amount of ricotta salata on top.

STYLING TIP

I like to use a Y-peeler to create thin shavings of cheese for my salads, not only because it looks nice, but because it allows the cheese to sort of melt in your mouth in contrast to crunchy ingredients like the Romanesco and hazelnuts.

celery and grapes with smoked almonds

My friend Hugh told me the man who created the celery juice diet came up with the idea in a dream. I don't know if it's true, but I do think that this salad is the stuff dreams are made of. Salty, savory, sweet, and it comes together in minutes. Celery leaves are maybe my favorite green: Delicate and full of celery flavor, they are also the most beautiful shade of pale green. Smoked almonds are a fun way to add lots of umami flavor and even more crunch. This is like the world's most elegant, deconstructed ants on a log.

PRODUCE

6 stalks celery, plus the leaves from the whole head

1 cup (150 g) grapes, halved

1 lemon

DAIRY

4 ounces (115 g) Manchego cheese (or Pecorino or Parmesan if you can't find Manchego)

PANTRY

1 (6-ounce/170 g) container smoked almonds

Extra-virgin olive oil (the good stuff)

Flaky salt

Pinch crushed red pepper flakes (optional)

PREP: Prepare an ice bath. Slice off the ends of 6 stalks celery on a diagonal and discard them. Shave the stalks on a mandoline, very thinly, about the thickness of a coin. Put the shavings right into the ice bath. Put the leaves from the whole head in there too. Let them crisp up for at least 10 minutes, then drain, dry them off, and transfer them to a large mixing bowl.

Cut 1 cup (150 g) grapes in half.

ASSEMBLE AND SERVE: Add the grapes to the bowl with the celery, and shave 4 ounces cheese using a Y-peeler (or grate with a mandoline, or just really, really thinly slice it) into the bowl. Chop up one 6-ounce (170 g) container smoked almonds with a serrated knife. Add them to the bowl and mix with a bit of good olive oil, flaky salt, lemon juice, and if you want to, some red pepper flakes. Transfer to a serving bowl, platter, or individual plates.

kale caesar

People are afraid of anchovies and raw egg yolks, but they love Caesar salad. Don't be afraid of these ingredients! This salad is easy to make with a few pantry items. Use the greens you prefer—it's also great with romaine, Little Gem, or escarole.

PRODUCE
1 clove garlic

2 lemons

1 bunch kale (I like Tuscan)

DAIRY
1 egg yolk

Parmesan cheese

PANTRY
2 cups (90 g) crusty bread torn into smallish pieces

Extra-virgin olive oil

Kosher salt and freshly ground black pepper

3 anchovies, plus a few boquerones (white anchovies) for serving if you'd like to be fancy

1 teaspoon Dijon mustard

COOK: Preheat the oven to 400°F (205°C). Place 2 cups (90 g) bread pieces on a rimmed baking sheet and drizzle with about 3 tablespoons oil. Squeeze the oil into the bread—really get in there and try to get it all soaked up. Sprinkle with salt. Grate a little bit of Parmesan over the top. Bake until the croutons are golden brown, 10 to 15 minutes, stirring halfway through.

MAKE THE REAL CAESAR DRESSING: Finely chop 3 anchovies and 1 clove garlic and then sprinkle about 1 teaspoon salt over this mixture. Using the side of your knife, smooth and mash the salt into the anchovies and garlic to create a paste.

In a medium bowl, whisk together the egg yolk, the zest of 1 lemon, about 2 tablespoons lemon juice, and 1 teaspoon mustard. In a smooth, steady stream—while whisking— slowly drizzle in about ¼ cup (60 ml) oil (you may need a little bit more). Add the anchovy mixture and whisk to combine. Taste and season with additional salt if required.

PREP: Remove the tough stems from 1 bunch kale and tear the leaves into bite-size pieces; wash and spin dry.

ASSEMBLE AND SERVE: Add the kale to the bowl with the dressing. Massage it a bit with clean hands, gently squeezing the dressing into the kale to tenderize it—just a couple of times. Add almost all of the croutons, toss, and then transfer the whole thing to a serving platter or plates. Top with the remaining croutons, plenty of Parmesan shavings, and fancy anchovies if you've got 'em. Serve with lots of lemon wedges on the side!

STYLING TIP

Torn croutons not only look "perfectly imperfect," but there's more surface area for browning and more nooks and crannies to collect little bits of dressing.

shredded kale and brussels with roasted squash and pomegranate

SERVES 2 TO 4 AS A STARTER OR SIDE, OR AS A FULL MEAL WITH A LITTLE PROTEIN

Sometimes a kale salad is just . . . too much kale. Finely shredded and used more as a condiment here, the kale's earthiness balances out the sweetness of the squash and creates a textual combination that I really enjoy. Besides bold flavors, this salad is full of vibrant fall colors and ready for any holiday table. It's easy to double the recipe for a larger crowd.

PRODUCE

1 delicata squash

6 cloves garlic, unpeeled

1 bunch Tuscan kale (about ½ pound/225 g)

½ pound (225 g) Brussels sprouts

Seeds from 1 pomegranate (about 1 cup/180 g)

DAIRY

Coconut or sheep's milk yogurt, for serving

PANTRY

Extra-virgin olive oil

Kosher salt and freshly ground black pepper

1 teaspoon honey

2 teaspoons grainy mustard

2 tablespoons apple cider vinegar

COOK: Preheat the oven to 425°F (220°C).

Cut 1 delicata squash into ¼-inch (6 mm) rings with a sharp knife. Use a spoon to scoop out the seeds. Spread the squash and 6 cloves garlic on a rimmed baking sheet. Drizzle with about 2 tablespoons oil, and season with salt and pepper. Toss to coat. Roast, tossing once, until golden brown on both sides, about 25 minutes.

PREP: Using a knife, remove the tough stems from 1 bunch kale, and the stem ends of ½ pound (225 g) Brussels sprouts. To shred the kale and Brussels sprouts, use the shredding attachment of a food processor. If you don't have a food processor, you can do this by hand, but it does take some time. You could use a mandoline for the Brussels, but really try to get that kale finely shredded too.

MAKE THE ROASTED GARLIC VINAIGRETTE: If you've used your food processor, rinse out the base to make the vinaigrette. Using the normal blade, squeeze the roasted garlic from their skins into the food processor and add 1 teaspoon honey, 2 teaspoons mustard, 2 tablespoons cider vinegar, 3 tablespoons oil, and plenty of salt and pepper. Process until smooth. If you don't have a food processor, you could use a blender for this part, or just mash the garlic with the side of your knife or with a mortar and pestle until it becomes a smooth paste, and then whisk in the other ingredients.

ASSEMBLE AND SERVE: Pour the dressing into a large bowl, and then add the shredded kale and Brussels sprouts and the seeds from 1 pomegranate. Toss to combine and check for seasoning. Letting this mixture sit for a few minutes will help tenderize the kale. Arrange the squash on a platter, then top with the kale mixture. Serve with yogurt on the side.

fall greens, apples, and cheddar

SERVES 4 AS A SIDE (THIS IS TURKEY OR HAM'S EXCITING, NEW BEST FRIEND.)

This salad combines some of the best things about fall on a single plate. There used to be a wonderful restaurant in Alphabet City when I lived there, Northern Spy, and I woke up early every weekend to stand in line and wait to get the kale and Cheddar salad and biscuits. Then I moved to Bed-Stuy and by some sort of miracle I was near Fancy Nancy, where they served the same salad. I could order it to go or sit at the bar and never have to wait in line. Put two fried eggs on top of this salad, and it could be brunch. Serve it with a side of biscuits with apple butter or maple butter and a cup of hot coffee and just forget it.

PRODUCE

½ pound (225 g) sweet potatoes

1 bunch kale

1 bunch Swiss chard

1 apple, something tart and crisp like a Granny Smith or Honey Crisp

1 lemon (optional)

DAIRY

¾ cup (about 85 g) sharp, crumbly, really good Cheddar (like Cabot clothbound), broken into pieces

PANTRY

Extra-virgin olive oil

Kosher salt and freshly ground black pepper

1 tablespoon grainy mustard

1 teaspoon real Vermont maple syrup (the darker the better, I think)

1 tablespoon apple cider vinegar

2 tablespoons toasted walnut or almond oil

½ cup (50 g) whole almonds, toasted (see page 20)

COOK: Preheat the oven to 425°F (220°C).

Slice ½ pound (225 g) sweet potatoes into ¼-inch (6 mm) rounds and toss with olive oil and salt and pepper on a rimmed baking sheet. Roast until deep golden brown on both sides, flipping once about halfway through, about 25 minutes.

PREP: Remove the stems of 1 bunch each of kale and chard, slice the leaves, and give everything a chop—it's hard to eat this if the greens are too much of a tangle.

MAKE THE GRAINY MUSTARD, MAPLE, AND APPLE CIDER VINAIGRETTE: Combine 1 tablespoon mustard, 1 teaspoon maple syrup, 1 tablespoon cider vinegar, and 2 tablespoons toasted walnut oil in a large bowl and season with salt and pepper.

ASSEMBLE AND SERVE: Add the greens to the dressing. Slice 1 apple (lemon juice can be used to prevent browning) and add it, along with the roasted sweet potatoes and ¾ cup (about 85 g) crumbled Cheddar. Toss together. Transfer to plates or a platter. Chop up ½ cup (50 g) toasted almonds and sprinkle on top.

sheet pan salad

While writing this book one evening, I walked over to my friends the Stevenses' house. They always feed us, and have the kombucha and snacks we like, and they are just the most welcoming and lovely hosts. One night they let us use their sauna, and Suze gave us big bowls of perfectly roasted vegetables (seriously the best—her secret is not moving them once they go in the oven!) and (veggie) sausage, and every evening after that I wanted this dish for dinner. It's warm, comforting, satisfying, doesn't make a huge mess, and hardly takes any time at all to make. The best part of all is that Ben makes it even better than I do, which is really a treat (because I pretty much always do the cooking). It's highly adaptable to what you have on hand, so check out the chart on page 263 for roasting times—remember to group ingredients with similar roasting times on baking sheets and not to overcrowd the pans!

PRODUCE

1 pound (455 g) Brussels sprouts, trimmed and halved

1 large head broccoli, cut into florets, or 1 bunch broccolini, trimmed

2 small sweet potatoes or 1 large, cut into ¼-inch-thick (6 mm) rounds

½ pound (225 g) small fingerling potatoes, halved

1 handful whatever green you have on hand (I love arugula or a chicory)

MEAT

1 (12-ounce/340 g) package of your favorite precooked sausage or veggie sausage—I love Seemore's La-Dolce-Beet-a or Hot Italian Chicken Sausage, cut on the diagonal into ¾-inch (2 cm) slices

PANTRY

¼ cup (35 g) golden raisins

¼ cup (60 ml) white balsamic vinegar

Extra-virgin olive oil

Kosher salt and freshly ground black pepper

1 tablespoon grainy mustard

PREP: Combine ¼ cup (35 g) golden raisins and ¼ cup (60 ml) white balsamic vinegar. Trim 1 pound (455 g) Brussels sprouts and cut them in half. Cut 1 head broccoli into florets. Slice 2 small or 1 large sweet potato into ¼-inch (6 mm) rounds. Cut ½ pound (225 g) fingerling potatoes in half.

COOK: Preheat the oven to 425°F (220°C).

On one sheet pan, combine the Brussels and broccoli, and on the other, combine the sweet potatoes, fingerling potatoes, and 1 package sliced sausage. Toss the ingredients on each pan with a drizzle of oil—about 2 tablespoons for each pan. Season really generously with salt and pepper.

Put the broccoli pan on the top rack and the potato pan on the bottom rack. Roast for 25 minutes and remove the broccoli pan if things are looking nice and browned. Give

the potato pan a good toss and roast until everything is deep golden brown, 10 to 15 more minutes.

FINISH THE RAISIN VINAIGRETTE: Add 1 tablespoon mustard and 2 tablespoons oil to the raisin-vinegar mixture, whisking to emulsify, and season well with salt and pepper.

ASSEMBLE AND SERVE: Spoon the roasted veggies and sausage over 1 handful greens on a platter or bowls and drizzle with a bit of raisin dressing.

crispy chickpea and avocado rice bowl

This is a deceptively simple salad. It doesn't seem like much at first glance at the ingredients, but it's a really flavorful and super-satisfying vegan meal.

PRODUCE

1 (3-inch/7.5 cm) piece ginger

2 limes

1 to 2 serrano chiles

2 heads Little Gem lettuce (or you could try romaine or butter lettuce)

2 avocados

1 bunch scallions

1 handful fresh cilantro leaves

PANTRY

2 teaspoons honey

2 tablespoons rice vinegar

¼ cup (60 ml) avocado oil (or other neutral oil)

Kosher salt

1 cup (190 g) black rice (or brown rice or quinoa, if preferred)

1 recipe Crispy Chickpeas (page 260)

PREP: Set a small pot of water to boil.

MAKE THE GINGER, LIME, AND CHILE VINAIGRETTE: Peel and grate 3 inches (7.5 cm) ginger into a small bowl using a Microplane. Add 2 teaspoons honey, the juice of 1 lime, 2 tablespoons rice vinegar, and ¼ cup (60 ml) avocado oil and season with salt. Whisk until combined. Thinly slice 1 to 2 chiles, removing the seeds if you don't want the heat, and stir into the vinaigrette.

COOK: Add 1 cup (190 g) black rice to the boiling water and cook for 20 minutes, then drain and return to the pot. (This timing will vary if you are using another grain.)

ASSEMBLE AND SERVE: Separate the leaves of 2 heads lettuce and tear into bite-size pieces; wash and spin dry. Arrange the lettuce leaves on a platter, and then add a bit of rice. Peel, pit, and thinly slice 2 avocados, and thinly slice 1 bunch scallions. Add the avocado pieces to the platter. Drizzle the lettuce and avocado with the dressing and then sprinkle with cilantro, scallions, and crispy chickpeas. Serve with lime wedges.

STYLING TIP
I sliced the avocado widthwise here for a different look—isn't it pretty this way?

gomae

This Japanese spinach salad always reminds me of Sobaya, one of my favorite restaurants in New York. Tucked away on Ninth Street, when you enter the warmly lit, crowded little space, it's like a passageway straight to Japan, and the city outside falls away with the first taste of steamy soba. Enjoy this simple and clean salad with a delicious noodle soup, sushi, or fish and rice. I see many recipes out there for shortcuts using tahini, but I love the texture of the sesame seeds crushed by hand, and it hardly takes any time at all, especially if you buy pretoasted sesame seeds.

PRODUCE	PANTRY
1 pound (455 g) spinach	Kosher salt
	¼ cup (40 g) plus 1 tablespoon toasted sesame seeds
	2 tablespoons soy sauce
	2 teaspoons honey
	2 teaspoons mirin

PREP: Trim the ends of the stems from 1 pound (455 g) spinach; wash the leaves well and spin dry.

COOK: Bring a large pot of heavily salted water to a boil. Prepare an ice bath. Add the spinach to the boiling water and cook it for just a minute or two, until the stems are just tender and it's bright green. Using a spider or tongs, transfer it immediately to the ice bath.

MAKE THE SESAME SOY DRESSING DRESSING: Using a mortar and pestle, crush ¼ cup (40 g) sesame seeds until they are mostly smooth but have a little texture left. Put them in a large bowl. Then, really crush 1 tablespoon sesame seeds until completely smooth—no full seeds or chunks should remain. Add to the large bowl. Stir in 2 tablespoons soy sauce, 2 teaspoons honey, and 2 teaspoons mirin.

ASSEMBLE AND SERVE: Drain the spinach in a fine-mesh sieve and press with a spatula to remove some of the water. Transfer to a clean kitchen towel that you don't mind getting quite dirty—and twist together at the top to form a bundle. Twist and squeeze with all of your might to get out the excess water. Mix the spinach and the sesame paste and serve.

play on a waldorf salad

SERVES 2 TO 4 AS A STARTER OR SIDE

This salad's subtle, sweet flavors, in my opinion, do not need to be enrobed in a thick layer of mayonnaise or whipped cream. I recommend keeping all the ingredients feeling fresh and beautiful without forgoing the richness by toasting your nuts in butter and serving with a nice, ripe, soft cheese. Riff on it even more if you like—use Granny Smith apples, add chicken, or try it with dates; but please, no marshmallows.

PRODUCE

1 clove garlic, smashed

2 stalks celery, plus the leaves from the whole head

1 head frisée

Juice of ½ lemon

1 large or 2 small Asian pears

1 cup (150 g) green seedless grapes

DAIRY

1 tablespoon best-quality unsalted butter

Camembert or another soft, ripe cheese

PANTRY

1 handful golden raisins

¼ cup (60 ml) Champagne vinegar

Kosher salt and freshly ground black pepper

1 big handful walnuts

Extra-virgin olive oil

1 tablespoon grainy mustard

Preheat the oven to 350°F (175°C).

START THE PICKLED RAISIN VINAIGRETTE: In a large bowl, combine 1 handful raisins, 1 clove smashed garlic, ¼ cup (60 ml) vinegar, and a pinch of salt.

COOK: Spread 1 big handful walnuts on a rimmed baking sheet with a drizzle of oil and 1 tablespoon butter. Season with salt and pepper and toast until fragrant and golden brown, about 8 minutes. Set a timer!

PREP: Thinly slice 2 stalks celery on the bias and then add it to a salad spinner filled with ice-cold water. Separate the leaves of 1 head frisée and tear into bite-size pieces; add to the salad spinner with the celery, moving around with your hand to knock off any dirt. Let sit for about 5 minutes to crisp up while you finish making the rest of the salad. Drain and spin everything dry before use.

FINISH THE PICKLED RAISIN VINAIGRETTE: Remove the garlic from the vinegar. Add 1 tablespoon mustard, the juice of ½ lemon, and about ¼ cup (60 ml) oil. Whisk together until combined and season with salt and pepper.

ASSEMBLE AND SERVE: Cut the cheeks off 1 large or 2 small Asian pears, then cut them into thin slices and add to the bowl with the dressing. Halve the grapes and put them in the bowl. Add the celery and frisée and toss everything to combine. Arrange on a platter and crush the toasted walnuts with your hand over the top. Add the cheese to the side of the plate.

crispy calamari with carrots, frisée, and ginger

This salad, paired with a grilled steak and an ice-cold martini or glass of white wine, is exactly what you would order at any restaurant any summer night in the Hamptons. Maybe you would start off with some oysters. Sure, if you were there instead of reading this, you might be sitting next to Billy Joel, but making it wherever you call home for guests or family just has to do sometimes, especially when your mom is a social liability after a single glass of Pinot Grigio on ice (yes, Mom, you're louder than you think, and they can hear you when you say something about their plastic surgery). This salad is inspired by a few salads I have had at restaurants in the Hamptons. I only wish I could somehow provide the same people-watching as the deck of the American Hotel.

PRODUCE
1 lime

2 small heads or 1 large head frisée

3 carrots

MEAT
1 pound (455 g) fresh cleaned calamari

PANTRY
1 recipe Citrusy Ginger Vinaigrette (see page 45)

Neutral oil

4 sheets graham crackers

1 cup (125 g) all-purpose flour

Kosher salt

Toasted sesame seeds

MAKE THE CITRUSY GINGER VINAIGRETTE: Follow the instructions on page 45.

PREP: Separate the leaves of 2 small heads or 1 large head frisée and tear into bite-size pieces; wash and spin dry. Peel 3 carrots and cut into julienne.

In a large heavy-bottomed pot, preheat 2 to 3 inches (5 to 7.5 cm) of oil to 350°F (175°C).

Grind 4 graham crackers in a food processor until they are uniform crumbs. In a large bowl, combine the crumbs, 1 cup (125 g) flour, and 1 teaspoon salt.

Cut the squid tentacles in half and cut the tube into ¼-inch (6 mm) rings. Toss the calamari in the flour mixture and give them a little shake in a mesh strainer to get the excess coating off.

COOK: Fry the calamari in batches, until deep golden brown—2 to 3 minutes. Transfer with a spider or slotted spoon to a paper towel–lined plate and sprinkle with salt.

ASSEMBLE AND SERVE: Toss the frisée and carrots in the dressing. I like to sprinkle the calamari on top, so the coating stays as crisp as possible. Sprinkle with sesame seeds and serve with lime wedges.

spoon salad for abdullah

When my friend Abdullah gets excited about something, it's impossible not to get excited about it as well. Eyes wide while he brainstormed on the hammock, enthusiastic about salads, he told me he used to drink dressing as a kid. Abdullah said that as a busy guy on the go, what he was interested in was a "Spoon Salad," something chopped up into small enough pieces he could just shovel it into his mouth as he was moving on to the next thing. This is the only chopped salad in the book, and the only one that can be eaten with a spoon.

PRODUCE

2 limes

1 (2-inch/5 cm) piece unpeeled ginger

½ head Napa cabbage

2 Persian cucumbers

½ small red onion

1 serrano or Thai chile

1 handful fresh basil

1 handful fresh cilantro

1 handful fresh mint

MEAT

1 boneless, skinless chicken breast

PANTRY

3 tablespoons fish sauce

3 tablespoons rice vinegar

2 teaspoons brown sugar

¼ cup (60 ml) avocado oil

Kosher salt

1 cup (85 g) unsweetened large coconut flakes

1 cup (240 ml) soy sauce

1 cup (150 g) roasted and salted redskin (skin-on) peanuts

MAKE THE THAI-STYLE VINAIGRETTE: In a large bowl, combine 3 tablespoons fish sauce, 3 tablespoons rice vinegar, the juice of 1 lime, 2 teaspoons brown sugar, and ¼ cup (60 ml) avocado oil. Season with salt if necessary (depends how salty your fish sauce is).

COOK: Preheat the oven to 350°F (175°C). Spread 1 cup (85 g) coconut on a rimmed baking sheet. Bake 8 to 10 minutes, stirring occasionally. Set aside.

Fill a small pot of water about one-third of the way. Add 1 cup (240 ml) soy sauce. Slice 1 lime and one 2-inch (5 cm) unpeeled piece ginger and add to the pot; bring to a boil. Reduce to a simmer and add the chicken breast. Poach for 12 to 15 minutes, until the chicken is cooked through (the temperature should reach 165°F/74°C). Remove the chicken from the water and let cool. Discard the poaching liquid. Once cool enough to handle, chop the chicken finely and add to the large bowl with the dressing.

PREP: Finely chop ½ head Napa cabbage, 2 Persian cucumbers, ½ red onion, 1 chile, and 1 handful each of basil, cilantro, and mint, adding to the bowl with the chicken as you go. Using a mandoline makes slicing the cabbage, cucumbers, and chile go faster, but it's not necessary since everything is getting chopped into spoon-size bits. I chop everything one at a time, so my cutting board doesn't get unwieldy.

Finely chop the coconut flakes and 1 cup (150 g) peanuts and add them to the bowl with the chicken and vegetables.

ASSEMBLE AND SERVE: Toss everything together with the dressing, then transfer to serving bowls—or just eat right out of the big bowl if you're not sharing. Eat with a spoon, even if you're not running out the door.

health food salad

SERVES 2 AS A MEAL

My friend Randi inspired this fridge-clean-out salad, but this also reminds me of the salads you find at a food coop salad bar or health food restaurant—in the best possible way. Feel free to add whatever you may have in the back of your refrigerator—limp celery or part of a head of fennel, thinly sliced on a mandoline, are very welcome.

PREP: Cut 1 head cabbage into quarters and remove a bit of the white core with a paring knife. Use your mandoline to shave the cabbage, very thinly, right into a big bowl. Use the julienne attachment to julienne 4 carrots, or you can use the bigger holes on a box grater.

ASSEMBLE AND SERVE: Toss in 2 handfuls sprouts, 1 cup (145 g) raisins, 1 cup (140 g) sunflower seeds, ¼ cup (40 g) hemp seeds, and 1 tablespoon poppy seeds. Toss with a big pinch of salt, a couple tablespoons oil, and start with the juice of ½ lemon, but you may need a bit more, depending on how big your cabbage was. Serve with lemon wedges.

PRODUCE

1 small head red cabbage

4 carrots

2 big handfuls mixed sprouts, such as pea shoots, lentils, radish, alfalfa

1 lemon

PANTRY

1 cup (145 g) raisins

1 cup (140 g) shelled roasted sunflower seeds

¼ cup (40 g) hemp seeds

1 tablespoon poppy seeds

Kosher salt

Extra-virgin olive oil

sweet potatoes, avocado, and roasted pumpkin seed oil

My friend Lauryn introduced me to the magic of pumpkin seed oil. It is a dark, viscous oil that looks like it would drip out of your car, but it's silky, rich, and absolutely decadent. It makes simple, steamed sweet potatoes an absolutely luxurious dish. Forget pumpkin spice; I feel like this oil's deep nuttiness and subtle sweetness may be the flavor embodiment of fall.

PRODUCE

4 medium sweet potatoes

2 avocados

Handful of baby mizuna or other spicy microgreens

PANTRY

Roasted pumpkin seed oil

Flaky salt

PREP: Halve 4 medium sweet potatoes and cut into 1-inch (2.5 cm) wedges.

COOK: Fill a large skillet, wide pot, or a wok with water about 1-inch (2.5 cm) up the sides. Lower a steamer basket into the pot and place as much of the sweet potato as you can inside (you will probably have to work in batches). Turn the heat to medium-high and cover the pot with a lid. Steam for about 15 minutes— you can poke the potatoes with a paring knife to make sure they're tender.

Let cool a bit before serving (as hot avocado weirds some people out).

ASSEMBLE AND SERVE: Slice 2 avocados. Arrange sweet potatoes and avocados on a platter and drizzle with a good amount of pumpkin seed oil—if a little pools on the bottom of the plate that's okay! Sprinkle with a handful of mizuna and some flaky salt and serve!

kabocha squash with herbs and cabbage

I love black garlic and I use it often; it is an aged garlic with a very unique, fermented, funky sweetness (think balsamic vinegar meets roasted garlic) that is a really beautiful complement to the roasty, toasty flavors of fall. I like to add it to my stocks and soups all fall as well. I have been seeing it available at more and more stores, but you can definitely purchase it online, like I did— I accidentally ordered two pounds of it from SOS Chefs after eating a weed gummy. Well, I'll certainly be set for a while!

COOK: Preheat the oven to 450°F (230°C).

Carefully cut the top and bottom off the kabocha squash and then cut it in half. Scoop out the seeds and cut the squash into wedges 1 inch (2.5 cm) thick. Spread out on a rimmed baking sheet, toss with a couple of tablespoons of oil, and season with salt and pepper. Roast, flipping once, until deep golden brown and tender, about 30 minutes.

MAKE THE BLACK GARLIC VINAIGRETTE: Remove the skin from 1 head black garlic and use a mortar and pestle to smooth it into a paste (you should have about 1 tablespoon paste). In a small bowl, whisk the black garlic paste, 1 teaspoon salt, 2 tablespoons oil, the juice of 1 lime, and 2 teaspoons fish sauce.

ASSEMBLE AND SERVE: Cut 1 head red cabbage in half or quarters, remove the core, and shred very finely with a mandoline or by hand. Arrange the cabbage on a platter, followed by the warm squash. Drizzle with the dressing, then sprinkle with 1 big handful mint and ½ cup (75 g) chopped peanuts.

PRODUCE

1 small kabocha squash

1 head black garlic

Juice of 1 lime

1 really small head red cabbage, or ½ large head

1 big handful fresh mint leaves

PANTRY

Avocado oil

Kosher salt and freshly ground black pepper

2 teaspoons fish sauce

½ cup (75 g) roasted and salted redskin (skin-on) peanuts

parsnips, parsley, and toasted buckwheat

SERVES 2 TO 4 AS A MAIN DISH

Beige parsnips are easy to ignore in contrast to bold, brightly colored carrots, but they are really one of the best flavors of fall. They taste sweet and herbaceous, and with toasty buckwheat and sweet fragrant pear they won't be overlooked again!

PRODUCE

5 medium parsnips

1 small red onion

Juice of 1 lemon

1 ripe pear such as Bosc, Bartlett, or Anjou

1 bunch fresh parsley

1 handful arugula, torn if adult

PANTRY

¼ cup (35 g) golden raisins

¼ cup (60 ml) white balsamic vinegar

1 cup (165 g) toasted buckwheat groats (kasha)

Kosher salt and freshly ground black pepper

Extra-virgin olive oil

½ cup (50 g) walnuts

PREP: Preheat the oven to 425°F (220°C). Get 1½ cups (680 ml) water boiling in a small pot.

In a small bowl, combine ¼ cup (35 g) golden raisins and ¼ cup (60 ml) vinegar.

COOK: Add 1 cup (165 g) kasha to the pot of boiling water, along with a big pinch of salt and a little drizzle of oil. Cook until tender with just a little tooth, 7 to 9 minutes. Transfer to a bowl and set aside to cool.

Peel 5 parsnips and cut them in half lengthwise, and then in half widthwise. Place them on a rimmed baking sheet. Peel and thinly slice 1 red onion from root to tip. Add it to the baking sheet with the parsnips, drizzle with a couple tablespoons of oil and season with plenty of salt and pepper.

Roast, flipping things around with a spatula once, until they are getting nice and brown, about 20 minutes. Add the ½ cup (50 g) walnuts to the pan and cook 8 to 10 more minutes—until the nuts are also fragrant and golden. Set a timer!

ASSEMBLE AND SERVE: Add the parsnips, onion, and walnuts to the bowl with the cooked kasha. Add the raisins and vinegar, the juice of 1 lemon, and a good drizzle of oil. Thinly slice 1 pear and add it to the bowl. Remove the stems from 1 bunch parsley and add the leaves and 1 handful arugula to the bowl, season with salt and pepper, and toss again.

celery root, fennel, and apple

When it starts to get cold in New York, I am a complete wimp. I run from the sidewalks into restaurants with a bright red face and a runny nose seeking shelter and warmth. I remember many nights traveling to the West Village and bursting into a warm and welcoming Frankie's Spuntino and having their celery root and fennel salad and a huge bowl of meatballs and remembering why it's worth living in such a cold, crazy place.

PRODUCE
1 head fennel

½ small red onion

1 small celery root

1 Granny Smith apple

2 cups (60 g) fresh parsley leaves

1 lemon

DAIRY
Pecorino cheese

PANTRY
Extra-virgin olive oil

Kosher salt and freshly ground black pepper

PREP: Prepare an ice bath. Trim the stalk off 1 head fennel and set aside—you'll want to use the fronds later. Cut the bulb in half, and then using a mandoline, slice the fennel very thinly, about the thickness of cardstock paper. Place the sliced fennel in the ice bath to crisp it up.

Cut ½ red onion in half lengthwise and carefully use the mandoline to thinly slice each quarter onion. Place the onion in the ice bath with the fennel to mellow out its flavor just a bit.

Peel 1 celery root with a Y-peeler and cut it into quarters. Thinly slice on the mandoline and place in a medium bowl. Cut the cheeks off 1 apple, avoiding the core, then cut off the remaining sides. Slice the apple pieces on the mandoline and put in the bowl with the celery root.

ASSEMBLE AND SERVE: Remove the fennel and red onion from the ice bath and pat dry with paper towels or a clean kitchen towel. Transfer to the bowl with the celery root and apple. Add 2 cups (60 g) parsley leaves, the zest and juice of 1 lemon, and a good drizzle of oil (about 3 tablespoons) and season well with salt and pepper. Use the Y-peeler to shave a good amount of Pecorino cheese to sprinkle over the entire salad. Sprinkle the fennel fronds over top.

roasted vegetables with horseradish goat cheese and challah croutons

SERVES 4 TO 6 AS A SIDE

Serve this with a tender brisket, a side of salmon, a perfectly roasted, lemony, garlicky chicken. Feel free to try other vegetables you might have on hand; just take a look at the chart on page 263 for timing.

PRODUCE

2 bunches small carrots

½ pound (225 g) small fingerling potatoes

1 pound (455 g) Brussels sprouts

4 shallots, peeled

1 head garlic

2 tablespoons grated fresh horseradish (or 1 tablespoon jarred horseradish)

2 lemons

½ cup (15 g) fresh dill

2 cups (60 g) fresh parsley leaves

DAIRY

5 ounces (140 g) goat cheese, at room temperature

PANTRY

Extra-virgin olive oil

Kosher salt and freshly ground black pepper

Everything Challah (page 257), torn into 1-inch (2.5 cm) pieces (2 cups/60 g)

PREP: Preheat the oven to 425°F (220°C).

Peel 2 bunches carrots and cut them in half lengthwise. Cut ½ pound (225 g) fingerling potatoes, 1 pound (455 g) Brussels sprouts, and 4 peeled shallots in half. Separate 1 head garlic into cloves.

COOK: On one rimmed baking sheet, toss the carrots with 2 tablespoons oil and season with salt and pepper. Make sure they have plenty of space between them! On a second rimmed baking sheet, toss the potatoes, Brussels sprouts, shallots, and garlic with 2 tablespoons oil and season with salt and pepper. I like to make sure the potatoes are cut side down, so they get very crispy.

Roast the vegetables for 25 minutes, then give them a little toss to see how they are doing. They should be deep golden brown and will need about 10 minutes longer.

When the veggies are done, add 2 cups (60 g) torn challah pieces to a rimmed baking sheet. I like to transfer all of the vegetables to one and allow them to cool down a bit and reuse the other, so I don't have to do as many dishes. Toast the challah until golden brown, 6 to 8 minutes. Let cool just a bit.

MAKE THE HORSERADISH GOAT CHEESE: In the bowl of a food processor, combine 5 ounces (140 g) goat cheese, 2 tablespoons fresh horseradish, the zest and juice of 1 lemon, ½ cup (15 g) dill, and salt and pepper to taste. Blend until whipped, smooth, and completely combined, scraping down the sides as necessary.

ASSEMBLE AND SERVE: Spread the goat cheese mixture on plates or a platter. Toss the roasted vegetables with 2 cups (60 g) parsley and the challah and arrange on the plates. Serve with the lemon wedges.

crudités
with tonnato

MAKES ABOUT 2 CUPS (0.5 L) TONNATO;
SERVES 8 TO 12 AS AN APPETIZER

Why does that taste so good? Everyone will ask. What is that? It's so familiar . . . It's tuna and mayonnaise and a little bit of lemon and it's really very delicious. Use it is a dip as I've used it here, spread it on sandwiches, smear it on the bottom of a plate under roasted vegetables. I love how it tastes with bitter fall chicories. It makes a very simple thing feel very, very elegant. It's important to use good-quality tuna in a jar here. Yes, it's expensive, but if you're just spooning tuna onto vegetables, it really has to be the best tuna.

PREP: In the bowl of a food processor, combine 1 jar tuna and all of the oil from the jar, 2 tablespoons mayonnaise, and the zest and juice of 1 lemon. Blend until smooth, taste for seasoning, and add salt and pepper.

ASSEMBLE AND SERVE: Transfer the tonnato to a serving vessel and drizzle with a bit of good olive oil and sprinkle with more fresh pepper. Serve with vegetables, and bonus points if you put everything on a big platter of ice.

PRODUCE

1 lemon

A selection of raw vegetables, for serving (I like to keep a monochromatic color palette. Pale greens and whites are beautiful—here I've used striking purples.)

PANTRY

1 (6.7-ounce/190 g) jar pole-caught tuna packed in oil, drained

2 tablespoons mayonnaise

Kosher salt and freshly ground black pepper

Drizzle of good extra-virgin olive oil

Miso Mushrooms and Caramelized
Onion with Farro and Herby Hazelnut
Sauce (page 250)

miso mushrooms and caramelized onion with farro and herby hazelnut sauce

SERVES 2 TO 4 AS AN APPETIZER

Like that rare, perfect fall day when you find yourself outside in a thick, soft sweater—the sun is shining and the breeze is brisk, as copper and ochre leaves drift to the ground, and you've got a warm cup of something in your hand. That is this dish, deeply savory, earthy, filling but with a little something as bright and fresh as a gust of wind.

PRODUCE

1 large yellow onion, peeled, halved, and thinly sliced

5 scallions, chopped

1 clove garlic, peeled and roughly chopped

1 jalapeño pepper, roughly chopped

1 cup (30 g) fresh cilantro leaves

1 lime

2 pounds (910 g) mixed wild mushrooms, such as maitake, oyster, and shiitake

DAIRY

2 tablespoons unsalted butter, at room temperature

4 large eggs

PANTRY

1 cup (200 g) farro

Extra-virgin olive oil

1/3 cup (45 g) hazelnuts, toasted (see page 20), chopped

2 tablespoons white miso

Kosher salt and freshly ground black pepper

COOK: Fill a medium pot with cold water. Add 1 cup (200 g) farro and cook according to the package instructions, because there are a few different kinds of farro out there. Cook until the farro is tender but a bit of tooth remains.

Meanwhile, get your caramelized onions going. In a large skillet, get a couple of tablespoons of oil heating up over medium-high heat. Add 1 thinly sliced onion, toss around a bit, and then let it sit for a few minutes. Stir occasionally and let it cook for about 20 minutes. Don't rush it! Add a little water if the bottom of the pan starts to get a little dark—you want to keep going until your onion is deep brown and very soft. Transfer onion to a plate.

MAKE THE HERBY HAZELNUT SAUCE: In a large bowl, combine the 5 chopped scallions, chopped garlic, chopped jalapeños, cilantro, hazelnuts, zest and juice of 1 lime, and 3 tablespoons oil. Season well with salt. Store any extra in an airtight container for up to 1 week.

MAKE THE MISO BUTTER: In a small bowl, combine 2 tablespoons softened butter with 2 tablespoons miso using a rubber spatula. Taste and see if you need to add a bit of salt—you probably will.

MAKE THE MUSHROOMS: Prepare 2 pounds (910 g) mushrooms. Make sure they are clean. If they have a bit of dirt on them, contrary to what you might have read, you actually can very briefly dunk them into cold water to knock the dirt off—just make sure you put them on a towel to dry them off before you cook them, and don't leave them in the water too long. Trim the stems of the shiitakes off and cut the caps into halves or quarters. Tear the oyster and maitake mushrooms into large bite-size pieces.

In a large skillet, add a tiny bit of oil over medium-high to high heat. Once it's shimmering, add *some* of the mushrooms. You'll have to cook them in batches, so they sauté, not steam. You're aiming for a deep golden brown, which will take about 6 minutes per batch. Transfer the cooked mushrooms to a plate as you go. Once they are all done, return them all to the pan with the miso butter, and toss until they are coated. Check for seasoning, add salt if necessary, and definitely add some pepper. Transfer the mushrooms to a plate. You'll use this pan again for your eggs.

MAKE THE EGGS: Just before serving, make your crispy eggs. Get the pan you used for the mushrooms heating over medium-high heat. There should be a little oil and butter left in there, but if there's not, just add a little bit more. Once it's shimmering, crack 2 eggs in. Sprinkle with a little salt and pepper and cook until the edges of the egg are crispy and the whites are opaque, about 3 minutes. Repeat with 2 more eggs.

ASSEMBLE AND SERVE: Divide the farro among four serving bowls and top with the caramelized onion and the mushrooms. Top each with a crispy egg and plenty of hazelnut sauce.

all about
dressings

This book is full of some of my favorite dressings, which I have compiled into an index (page 255), categorized by style. While the recipes offer clear guidance, here are some general rules for how to make, store, dress, and serve your dressings:

1   It's important to taste dressings for seasoning and balance them to your liking. The idea of measuring out tablespoons of citrus juice is crazy to me, but there are giant lemons and tiny ones, so some of these recipes may require a little more oil than I call for, or a little more salt than you're used to. Getting used to tasting as you go is a great skill in the kitchen. Practice it enough and you will be able to eyeball dressing ingredients in no time.

2   I usually like to make only as much of a vinaigrette or dressing as is needed for a recipe because some flavors can get bitter, can intensify, or just are not quite as tasty after sitting too long. But if there is a dressing you love, you can try to double, triple, or quadruple the recipe and keep it in your fridge—most should keep for about a week (other than the Green Goddess Dressing, page 262, which will discolor).

3   Make sure your lettuce and other ingredients are dried well after washing, as dressings won't coat wet things as well.

4   Never dress a salad until it's ready to serve, unless the recipe instructs you to! If you're traveling somewhere, it's best to assemble your salad at the party. Always air on the side of underdressing—and add a little at a time.

5   I like to serve creamy dressings on the side, drizzle them on top, or swoop them on the bottom of the plate for visual appeal (this also minimizes the potential of overdressing and creating a soggy mess).

invent your own

If you want to experiment and make your own vinaigrettes, you can simply use the following basic formula, combining acid, oil, and whatever extra ingredients sound good to you. Feel free to get creative.

1 part acid +

BALSAMIC VINEGAR
BROWN RICE VINEGAR
CHAMPAGNE VINEGAR
CIDER VINEGAR
LEMON JUICE
LIME JUICE
ORANGE JUICE
RED WINE VINEGAR
SHERRY VINEGAR
WHITE BALSAMIC
    VINEGAR
WHITE WINE VINEGAR
UME (PLUM) VINEGAR
UNSEASONED RICE
    VINEGAR

3 parts oil +

EXTRA-VIRGIN OLIVE OIL
GRAPESEED OIL
SAFFLOWER OIL
SESAME OIL
SUNFLOWER OIL
WALNUT OIL

extras

ANCHOVIES (mashed)
BLUE CHEESE
BUTTERMILK
CITRUS ZEST
CORIANDER SEEDS
CUMIN SEEDS
DIJON MUSTARD
EGG YOLK
FENNEL SEEDS
FRESH HERBS
GARLIC (grated)
GINGER (grated)
HONEY MAPLE SYRUP
MAYONNAISE
MISO
PARMESAN (grated)
PICKLES
SESAME SEEDS
SHALLOT (minced)
SOY SAUCE
SUGAR
TAHINI
WHOLE-GRAIN MUSTARD

Whether you are in the mood for tangy vinaigrettes or creamy dressings, use these recipes found throughout the book when you are ready to make your own salads.

tangy

creamy

briny

When preserving, especially fermenting, make sure you use a sterile, airtight jar. Visit Ball's website (freshpreserving.com) to read up on all the preserving steps—it has everything you need to know to make sure you're preserving safely. If you ever notice any mold or other sign that something doesn't seem right, it's not. And I always keep my ferments in the fridge after the initial few weeks.

quick-pickled chive blossoms

MAKES ABOUT 1 CUP (160 G)

This is not only a beautiful way to preserve chive blossoms a little longer than the one week of spring they are in season, but the blossoms give a mild oniony flavor to vinegar and infuses it with an incredibly vibrant magenta hue.

 1½ cups (360 ml) distilled white vinegar

 1 cup (160 g) chive blossoms

Bring 1½ cups (360 ml) vinegar to a boil in a small pot. Pour over 1 cup (160 g) chive blossoms in an airtight jar. Store in the refrigerator for a few days before using, and then you can keep them in the fridge for about 1 month.

lacto-fermented fresno chiles

MAKES ABOUT 2 CUPS (240 G)

I don't know what I would do if I didn't have these in my refrigerator. They kick all hot sauces to the curb, in my opinion.

 1 pound (455 g) Fresno chiles

 1 cup (240 ml) warm water

 1½ tablespoons (25 g) kosher salt

I recommend wearing gloves while you cut the peppers, so you don't accidentally rub your eye or anything else later in the day. I also recommend slicing them on a mandoline. But however you do it, slice up 1 pound (455 g) peppers and put them in a sterilized pint jar.

Whisk together 1 cup (240 ml) warm water and 1½ tablespoons (25 grams) salt until the salt is completely dissolved. Pour over the chiles and top with a fermenting weight, so the chiles don't float to the surface. Place a lid on top, leaving it loose. You want the fermentation gasses to be able to escape while keeping creatures (bugs, flies) out. A couple of layers of cheesecloth also work here.

Let the jar sit in a cool, dark place for 4 weeks. You might notice a few small bubbles in the jar; at this point taste a chile—it should be wonderfully tangy and bright. Store in the refrigerator for about 3 months.

everything challah with good olive oil and local honey

MAKES 2 LOAVES

It's a little indulgent to use ½ cup (120 ml) of really beautiful olive oil here, but it's also really worth it, because the flavor is simply divine.

- 3¾ teaspoons active dry yeast (about 1½ packages)
- 1 tablespoon plus ½ cup (15 ml plus 120 ml) local honey
- 1¾ cups (420 ml) lukewarm water about 110°F (43°C)
- ½ cup (120 ml) really good-quality fruity extra-virgin olive oil, plus some for greasing the bowl and cookie sheet
- 4 large eggs, plus one for the egg wash
- 1 tablespoon kosher salt
- 8 cups (1 kg) all-purpose flour, plus more for dusting
- Everything Seasoning and flaky sea salt

In a large bowl, or the bowl of an electric stand mixer (it has to be the big one!) dissolve 3¾ teaspoons yeast and 1 tablespoon honey in 1¾ cups (420 ml) lukewarm water; set aside for about 5 minutes, or until it starts to get foamy.

Whisk ½ cup (120 ml) oil into the yeast mixture, then beat in 4 eggs, one at a time, along with ½ cup (120 ml) honey and 1 tablespoon salt. Gradually add 8 cups (1 kg) flour about a cup at a time. When the dough starts coming together, turn out onto a floured work surface to knead by hand, or use the dough hook attachment on your mixer (it really strains the machine, but it can technically do it). Knead until the dough is nice and smooth, as my friend Sam would say, like a little baby.

Clean out whatever big bowl you made the dough in and grease it with a little oil and return the dough to the bowl. Cover with plastic wrap and let rise in a warm place for 1 hour, until almost doubled in size. (Or put it in the fridge overnight and continue in the morning if you want flavors to further develop. If you do this, bring it to room temperature before proceeding.) Punch down the dough, cover, and let rise again in a warm place for another 30 minutes.

Divide the dough in half (you can do this with a scale, but I never do), and take half the dough and form it into 6 equal-ish balls. Roll each ball into a foot-long strand. Place the 6 strands in a row, parallel to one another. Pinch the tops of the strands together. Move the outside right strand over two strands. Then take the second strand from the left and move it to the far right. Take the outside left strand and move it over two. Move the second strand from the right over to the far left. Start over with the outside right strand. Continue this until all strands are braided. For a straight loaf, tuck ends underneath. Repeat with the other half of the dough. Place the braided loaves on a greased cookie sheet with at least 2 inches (5 cm) in between.

Beat 1 egg and brush it on the loaves. Let the loaves rise for 1 hour.

Preheat the oven to 375°F (190°C) and brush the loaves again with the egg wash. Sprinkle the bread with Everything Seasoning and flaky salt and bake in the middle of the oven for 30 to 40 minutes, until golden. (If you have an instant-read thermometer, you can take out the challah when the bread hits an internal temperature of 190°F/88°C.) Cool the loaves on a rack.

focaccia bread

MAKES 1 LOAF

There is nothing, absolutely nothing, like fresh focaccia fresh out of the oven. Feel free to get creative with your toppings.

- 3¼ cups (415 g) all-purpose flour
- 1 tablespoon kosher salt
- 1¾ cups (420 ml) warm water (about 98°F/37°C)
- ½ teaspoon active dry yeast
- 1 tablespoon honey
- Extra-virgin olive oil
- Flaky salt

In a large bowl, combine 3¼ cups (415 g) flour and 1 tablespoon salt. Set aside.

Once I heard Mario Batali describe the ideal temperature for foaming yeast as the temperature of blood, but I like to think of it as a hot tub. In a glass measuring cup, combine 1¾ cups (420 ml) warm water, ½ teaspoon yeast, and 1 tablespoon honey. Give a good stir to dissolve the honey, and let the yeast get a bit foamy (which may take 5 or 10 minutes). Pour into the flour mixture and stir everything together. You don't really have to knead here—just do your best to combine everything, and you don't want any big dry patches (the dough will be quite wet).

Once everything is combined, pour ¼ cup (60 ml) oil into a clean big bowl (it can be the same one you mixed in, cleaned out), and make sure it's coating all of the sides. Then put in your dough, cover it with plastic wrap, and pop it into the fridge. It's best if you can wait 2 full days before proceeding, but at least wait overnight.

Bring out the dough and get a little oil on a quarter sheet pan (9 by 13 inches/23 by 33 cm) and then transfer the dough onto the pan. Use your fingers to sort of pull and stretch it into place to fill the pan. Cover it and keep it in a warm place. It might not quite double in size, but you want it to fill out the pan and be quite fluffy and room temperature. This completely depends on the temperature of your kitchen, but it will take at least 30 minutes, and could take up to a couple hours; don't rush it!

Preheat the oven to 450°F (230°C) with a rack positioned closest to the heating element (you can also preheat with a pizza stone if you have one). Like you're playing a wonky piano, gently use your fingers to dimple (but don't poke all the way through!) the dough all over its surface. Drizzle the dough with more oil—don't be stingy! Sprinkle with flaky salt. Bake until a beautiful deep golden brown, about 15 to 20 minutes, or until internal temperature reaches 110°F (74°C). Cool just a few minutes and remove the loaf from pan and set on a rack to cool.

garlicky buttermilk ranch dressing

MAKES ½ CUP (120 ML)

Because it tastes better than the stuff in the bottle, and it didn't come out of a bottle.

- ¼ cup plus two tablespoons (90 ml) mayonnaise
- ¼ cup (60 ml) buttermilk
- 1 tablespoon plus 1 teaspoon (15 ml) distilled white vinegar
- Pinch garlic powder
- Kosher salt and freshly ground black pepper

Put all of the ingredients in a small bowl and whisk to combine. The dressing keeps for about 1 week in the fridge.

lemony yogurt vinaigrette

MAKES ½ CUP (120 ML)

Creamy and rich but extremely bright, this dressing still feels surprisingly clean and fresh. Use a regular lemon in place of a Meyer if you can't find one!

- ⅓ cup (75 ml) regular yogurt (not Greek style)
- 3 tablespoons mayonnaise
- Zest of 1 Meyer lemon
- 1 clove garlic, grated
- Kosher salt and freshly ground black pepper

In a small-ish bowl, whisk together ⅓ cup (75 ml) yogurt, 3 tablespoons mayonnaise, the zest of 1 Meyer lemon, and 1 clove grated garlic. Season with salt and pepper. The dressing keeps for about 1 week in the fridge.

homemade ricotta

MAKES ABOUT 1 PINT (480 ML)

"Is it worth it?" you may be asking yourself, and the answer is yes. Homemade ricotta just tastes fresh; it's so light and a whole different thing than what you are able to buy in most stores. Try to buy good-quality organic milk and cream; if you're going to do it, do it.

- 2 quarts (2 L) organic whole milk
- 1 cup (240 ml) organic heavy cream
- 1 teaspoon Himalayan pink sea salt
- ¼ cup (60 ml) fresh lemon juice (from 2 small lemons), or more if needed

Run a piece of cheesecloth under water for a moment to dampen it and drape it over a fine-mesh sieve set over a large bowl.

In a medium pot, slowly bring 2 quarts (2 L) milk, 1 cup (240 ml) cream, and 1 teaspoon Himalayan salt to a gentle boil. Be careful not to scorch the milk—don't walk away! Check the temperature with an instant-read thermometer to make sure it reaches 200°F (93°C).

Remove the pot from the heat. Add ¼ cup (60 ml) lemon juice and stir to combine. Let sit for about 10 minutes. You should see the milk separate into clumpy milk curds. If it hasn't, add another tablespoon of lemon juice and wait a few more minutes.

Carefully pour the liquid through the cheesecloth and allow it to drain until all the liquid has passed through and you have a glorious basket of soft cheese. This can take up to 1 hour. Enjoy immediately or transfer to a container and refrigerate until ready to use. It will keep for about 3 days.

bacon, snoop-style

I was mesmerized, I was shocked, I was anxious as I watched Snoop from the television monitor in the back kitchen as he dumped strips of bacon into a hot pan, piled up on top of each other in a big clump. He swirled it around occasionally with a pair of tongs while he talked. I had always laid each strip flat, neatly fitting them in the pan, sometimes having to make multiple batches. But he dumped the bacon onto a paper towel–lined plate, and I saw how perfectly crispy and extra curly it was. I have never made bacon the old way again.

> **1 pound (455 g) of your favorite bacon (something not too thick-cut works best)**

Heat a cast-iron or other large skillet over medium heat, and dump the bacon in. Stir it around occasionally until curly and very crispy, 15 to 20 minutes. Transfer to a paper towel–lined plate.

chili crisp

MAKES 1¾ CUPS (420 ML)

Chili crisp is truly a secret weapon. Just enough heat and lots of texture; it's umami, and it's perfect on almost everything.

> **3 small shallots**
>
> **2 heads garlic, cloves separated (about 30)**
>
> **1½ cups (360 ml) safflower or peanut oil**
>
> **1 (3-inch/7.5 cm) piece ginger**
>
> **¼ cup (18 g) crushed red pepper flakes**
>
> **1 tablespoon honey**
>
> **2 tablespoons soy sauce**
>
> **¼ teaspoon ground cinnamon**

Peel and thinly slice 3 shallots and the cloves from 2 heads garlic on a mandoline. They should be thinner than a coin. Add the shallots and garlic to a small pot with 1½ cups (360 ml) oil. Simmer over medium heat for 15 to 20 minutes. You want them to be deep golden brown, but not too brown (they will start to become bitter!).

Meanwhile, peel a 3-inch (7.5 cm) piece ginger. Using a Microplane, grate into a small heatproof bowl (you should have about 2 tablespoons), then add ¼ cup (18 g) red pepper flakes, 1 tablespoon honey, 2 tablespoons soy sauce, and ¼ teaspoon cinnamon.

Carefully strain the pot of garlic and shallots through a fine-mesh sieve over the bowl. Let the crispy bits continue to crisp up on a paper towel–lined plate, and let your oil sit until it cools to room temperature, then combine the oil and crisp bits. Store in the fridge for about 1 month.

crispy chickpeas

MAKES ABOUT 2 CUPS (105 G)

Like croutons, only full of protein and packed with nutty flavor.

> **1 (15½-ounce/439 g) can chickpeas, drained and rinsed**
>
> **Extra-virgin olive oil**
>
> **Kosher salt**
>
> **Ancho chile powder (optional)**

Preheat the oven to 425°F (220°C) with a rimmed baking sheet inside.

Lay some paper towels or a clean dish towel on another rimmed baking sheet and add 1 can drained and rinsed chickpeas to the baking sheet, wiggle them around a bit, and pat them with another towel or paper towel and make sure they are very, very dry (this helps them become super crispy, and prevents them from flying all over your oven).

Carefully remove the preheating pan from the oven. Add a few tablespoons oil and the chickpeas and season well with salt and a few pinches of ancho chile powder, if using. Return to the oven and roast until deep golden brown and crispy, about 20 minutes, tossing once.

You can store the chickpeas for about a day in a sealed glass jar with plenty of headroom, or leave at room temperature in a bowl covered with a paper towel, but they're best enjoyed right away.

frizzled shallots

MAKES 1¼ CUPS (135 G)

Okay, I know I've already called a few things "secret weapons," but frizzled shallots are really magical. They are addictive. They make something ordinary spectacular. Super crunchy with a mellowed onion taste, try them on everything, not just salads.

    5 small shallots
    Vegetable oil
    Kosher salt

Use a mandoline to thinly slice 5 shallots into rings—they should be just about the thickness of a coin. Using a mandoline ensures that the rings are an even thickness and will cook at the same rate. If cutting by hand, try to make them as even as possible and watch for quicker-cooking pieces when you're frying.

Put the shallots in a small saucepan and add oil just to cover (I know this seems like a lot, but you'll use the shallot oil in recipes too). Cook the shallots over medium heat until they are deep golden brown, moving them about occasionally with a fork, 15 to 18 minutes. Carefully strain the

oil through a fine-mesh sieve into a heat-safe container and set aside to cool. Transfer the shallots to a paper towel–lined plate and sprinkle with salt.

Shallots will keep for 3 days in an airtight container. Store the oil in an airtight container up to 3 weeks. Use it for cooking or in other dressings; it will have a mild shallot flavor.

dukkah

MAKES ¾ CUP (110 G)

This Egyptian spice blend adds flavor and crunch to everything. It's the perfect thing to have on hand for when your salad (or whatever you're making) just needs a little something else but you can't figure out what. Don't like hazelnuts? That's okay— use whatever nut you like or have on hand; this is just my favorite combination.

    ½ cup (70 g) hazelnuts, roughly chopped
    2 tablespoons poppy seeds
    2 tablespoons hulled hemp seeds
    1 tablespoon whole coriander seeds
    1 tablespoon fennel seeds
    1 teaspoon cumin seeds

Preheat the oven to 350°F (175°C).

Put all of the ingredients on a small rimmed baking sheet. Bake for 6 to 8 minutes, until fragrant and toasty. Let cool completely. If desired, use a mortar and pestle, spice grinder, mini food processor, or even a large heavy skillet to crush the spice blend a little. If you like more texture, this won't be necessary.

rose petal za'atar

MAKES ABOUT ½ CUP (90 G)

Rose can be too floral and overpowering, but when it's used just right, it is lovely and luxurious. Petals are beautiful, less perfumy tasting than rosewater, and here I've balanced them with fresh herbs. This za'atar is something really special to sprinkle on salads (and almost anything else).

- ¼ cup (75 g) toasted sesame seeds
- 1 tablespoon ground sumac
- 2 tablespoons torn fresh mint leaves
- 2 tablespoons torn fresh parsley leaves
- 1 tablespoon crushed dried pink rosebuds

Combine all of the ingredients in a small bowl. Store in an airtight container in the fridge for about 1 week.

green goddess dressing

MAKES ABOUT 1¼ CUPS (300 ML)

If you'd prefer this to be vegan, substitute the buttermilk for ½ cup (120 ml) water and 1 to 2 tablespoons apple cider vinegar.

- 1 ripe avocado, pitted and peeled
- ½ cup (120 ml) buttermilk
- 1 cup (15 g) fresh basil leaves
- ½ cup (10 g) fresh dill, tough stems removed
- ½ cup (4 g) fresh mint leaves
- 2 cloves garlic, peeled
- Juice of ½ lemon
- Kosher salt and freshly ground black pepper

Put all of the ingredients except salt and pepper in a high-powered blender or a food processor. Blend until combined, scraping down the sides as necessary. Season with salt and pepper.

Store in an airtight container for up to 2 days—it will probably get a bit brown on the surface; just scrape this off or mix it in.

how to roast vegetables

Personally, I could live off of roasted vegetables alone. It's just the truth. The key to making them delicious is not skimping on extra-virgin olive oil and giving whatever you're roasting plenty of space on the baking sheet to let steam escape. Season with salt. Make sure you flip everything halfway through roasting. You can roast vegetables together if they have similar cooking times, but otherwise, be mindful of mixing.

All timing below is for a 425°F (220°C) oven.

> **ASPARAGUS: 15–20 minutes**
>
> **BEETS (whole in foil packet; see Note following): 60 minutes**
>
> **BROCCOLI (florets): 20–30 minutes**
>
> **BRUSSELS SPROUTS (halved): 20–30 minutes**
>
> **CABBAGE (wedges): 30–40 minutes**
>
> **CARROTS (halved if large): 30–40 minutes**
>
> **EGGPLANT (sliced): 25–30 minutes**
>
> **FENNEL (sliced): 25–30 minutes**
>
> **GARLIC (whole head): 35–40 minutes**
>
> **MUSHROOMS: 20–25 minutes**
>
> **ONIONS (sliced): 20–25 minutes**
>
> **PARSNIPS (halved if large): 30–40 minutes**
>
> **PEPPERS (strips): 20–25 minutes**
>
> **POTATOES (wedges): 30–40 minutes**
>
> **SWEET POTATOES (rounds): 35–40 minutes**
>
> **TOMATOES (cherry or grape): 20–25 minutes**
>
> **ZUCCHINI (rounds): 15–20 minutes**

Note: Make roasting packets for whole, skin-on beets. If there are multiple colors, you will make separate little packets for each, so the colors don't bleed into each other. To make a packet, line a piece of foil large enough to hold your beets with parchment paper. Place the beets in the center and sprinkle with orange zest and plenty of salt and pepper, and drizzle with a bit of olive oil. Bring the two opposite sides of the foil to meet. Fold the edges down about 1 inch (2.5 cm) and then fold again to create a nice, tight seal. Fold up the remaining edges a couple of times to finish your packet. Place your packets on a rimmed baking sheet and roast.

how to boil eggs

Prepare an ice bath.

In a medium pot over medium-high heat, boil water. Carefully lower eggs right from the fridge into the boiling water. Cook for 3 minutes for soft boiled, 6 to 7 minutes for jammy yolks, 11 minutes for a "perfect" boiled egg, and 13 minutes for all-the-way-cooked-through eggs.

Place eggs in an ice bath. Let cool completely, then remove from the ice bath. Roll eggs all over the counter with a bit of pressure to make small cracks that should help to cleanly peel off the shells for perfect eggs.

Martha Stewart, to say you have been a huge inspiration is an understatement. I learn something new from you every single time I'm around you. You've taught me never to take shortcuts on the path to doing anything. You are a true force and do it all with grace and style.

Linda Pugliese, for suggesting that test shoot that winter's day so long ago and inspiring me to create. I've been looking for a collaborator for a long time, and I thank you for sharing your ability to capture beauty, for calming my nerves, and for traveling across the country during a pandemic to make all of this happen. It's never been so easy to work with someone. You made this book come to life.

I have loved every minute of working with Sarah Smith, my agent. Thank you for believing in me and this project and all of your guidance—I have felt completely supported from our first phone call, and you are so on top of everything it allowed me to just make this book (in two months).

Laura Dozier, Deb Wood, and everyone at Abrams, I loved making this book with you.

Brett Long, who stood by my side in the kitchen, washing every lettuce leaf, keeping me sane, making things beautiful, and treating this project like his own—I cannot thank you enough. Laura Huang and Eden Bakti, and Clare Langan. And Laura Manzano who tested these salads.

It took a lot of encouragement and listening to get me here, and I could write another book on how grateful I am to have really good people in my life— Glennis Meagher, Hugh Jernigan, Jason Schreiber, Dan Deacon, David Malosh, Ionut Gitan, Omega, Lauryn Tyrell, Nathan Kloke, Shira Bocar, Pearl Jones, Greg Lofts, Imogen Lee, Molly Wenk, Jo Zazlof, Anand Wilder, and Brad Leone. And my LA family— the Stevenses, all of the Sinclairs, the Fishmans, the Hubers, the Lyons, Mimi + Michael, Hannah Olsen, and my new muse Benny Blanco. I love you all.

Thank you, Dawn Perry, Laurie Woolever, Sam Seneviratne, Sarah Mastracco, Julia Sherman,

Aran Goyoga, Lucinda Scala Quinn, Carla Lalli Music, Yewande Komolafe, and of course Christine Albano for the support, advice, and being such positive, kind, and talented women, giving me opportunities along the way and teaching me a lot.

My whole Martha Stewart family—Sarah Carey and Thomas Joseph, your tough love and high standards drove me to this book instead of madness. To the whole kitchen and every person who was part of creating something beautiful and allowed me to soak it in, cleaned up my messes, and kept hiring me. And Dorian and Heather.

To my actual family—Mom, Dad, Gary. Thanks for supporting whatever timeline I'm on. Dad, thanks for reminding me to breathe.

Thank you Daniel Friedman, for my first garden, for your encouragement and everything you did to lift me up—I appreciate all of it.

Dr. Calico, Danielle Keita-Taguci, and Liza Roekl, you have had the challenging job of keeping my mind, body, and spirit together—which was no easy feat.

Thank you, Jen Fiore, Nina Lalli at MONDAYS for your ceramics, FIG Earth Supply for getting my LA garden growing, and LettuceGrow, for my hydroponic garden.

Thank you, David Sedaris, I listened to your audiobooks as my nighttime ritual while writing, and I think I became a better writer through osmosis.

Ben Sinclair, I love you so much, Smoothie. You are a wild man, and it certainly hasn't been boring. I have grown through the journey and I am so happy to be here now with you. Thank you for the shared experiences, the house, the new beginning, the honesty, for trying, for squeezing me, for tasting every single salad, and for helping me push through my fear-based mindset so I can just keep making things beautiful. You inspire me all the time and make me laugh like no one else on earth.

index

Editor: Laura Dozier
Designer: Deb Wood
Design Manager: Heesang Lee
Managing Editor: Annalea Manalili
Production Manager: Larry Pekarek

Library of Congress Control Number: 2021946827

ISBN: 978-1-4197-5839-3
eISBN: 978-1-64700-691-4

Printed and bound in the United States
10 9 8 7 6 5 4

The material contained in this book is presented only for informational and artistic
purposes. If you use plants or flowers for any of the recipes included in this book we
suggest you use only items from farmers' markets or grocery stores. If you choose to
eat plants or flowers you may have found in the wild, you are doing so at your own
risk. The author has made every effort to provide well researched, sufficient, and
up-to-date information; however, we also urge caution in the use of this information.
The publisher and author accept no responsibility or liability for any errors, omissions,
or misrepresentations expressed or implied, contained herein, or for any accidents,
harmful reactions, or any other specific reactions, injuries, loss, legal consequences,
or incidental or consequential damages suffered or incurred by any reader of this
book. Readers should seek health and safety advice from physicians and safety
professionals.

Abrams books are available at special discounts when purchased in quantity for
premiums and promotions as well as fundraising or educational use. Special editions
can also be created to specification. For details, contact specialsales@abramsbooks.
com or the address below.

Abrams® is a registered trademark of Harry N. Abrams, Inc.

ABRAMS The Art of Books
195 Broadway, New York, NY 10007
abramsbooks.com